A

TREATISE ON THE LAW

RELATING TO THE

CUSTODY OF INFANTS.

A

TREATISE ON THE LAW

RELATING TO THE

CUSTODY OF INFANTS,

IN CASES OF DIFFERENCE BETWEEN

PARENTS OR GUARDIANS.

BY

WILLIAM FORSYTH,

OF THE INNER TEMPLE, ESQ., BARRISTER AT LAW, AND LATE FELLOW OF
TRINITY COLLEGE, CAMBRIDGE.
AUTHOR OF "A TREATISE ON COMPOSITION WITH CREDITORS."

LONDON:
WILLIAM BENNING & CO., LAW BOOKSELLERS,
43, FLEET STREET.

1850.

LONDON:
PRINTED BY RAYNER AND HODGES,
109, Fetter Lane, Fleet Street.

CONTENTS.

CHAPTER I.

CHAPTER II.

CHAPTER III.

CHAPTER IV.

CHAPTER V.

TABLE OF CASES.

THE LAW

RELATING TO

CUSTODY OF INFANTS.

———◆———

CHAPTER I.

THE RIGHTS OF PARENTS AND JURISDICTION OF COURTS IN QUESTIONS OF CUSTODY.

§ 1. THE state of the law relating to the custody of the persons of infants is not very satisfactory. Not only are there defects which can, perhaps, be remedied only by the authority of the Legislature; but there prevails an uncertainty in the application of the law, as it exists, to the difficult cases which frequently arise in connection with the disposal of minor children. This is owing in a great measure to the fact, that in the exercise of their jurisdiction in the matter, which, to use the words of Mr. Justice Story (a), "is

(a) Equity Jurisprudence, § 1342.

B

admitted to be of extreme delicacy and of no
inconsiderable embarrassment and responsibility,"
Courts of Equity and Common Law find that much
is necessarily left to their *discretion*, which varies
according to the circumstances of each particular
case.

The object of the following pages is to present
in a convenient compass the view which in
modern times those courts seem disposed to take
of the frequently conflicting wishes and claims of
parents or guardians, when family differences
unhappily occur, or other circumstances exist,
which call for the interference of judicial authority.

First, however, it may be not without interest,
and, perhaps, utility, to consider the view which
has been taken in other countries of the legal
rights of parents over their children.

§ 2. The Roman law was distinguished for the
stern severity with which it upheld the paternal
authority. It gave the father, in fact, absolute
power. *Jus autem potestatis, quod in liberos habemus,
proprium est civium Romanorum. Nulli enim alii
sunt homines qui talem in liberos habeant potestatem,
qualem nos habemus* (b). According to Dionysius

(b) Inst. i. 9, § 2. See Heinecc. Elem. Jur. Civ. Pandect.
tit. vi. § 143, *et seq.* Vinnius in Institut. p. 45, says, *Romanorum in liberos potestas neque finem habuit, nec modum.* And
where a father brought an action to recover possession of his son,
he claimed him *ex jure Romano* or *ex lege Quiritium*, Dig. vi. i. 2.

the historian, the atrocious power of putting his
children to death, and of selling them three times
in open market, was vested in the father from the
earliest times of the republic (*c*). But whatever
may have been the case previously, we know that
this right was recognised by the Twelve Tables,
and continued to be the law for many ages (*d*).
We find, however, that long before the reign of
Justinian it had been very considerably modified.
Bynkershoek is of opinion that the power of life
and death in the father began to grow into disuse
in the reign of the Emperor Hadrian (*e*), of whom
it is recorded that he banished a man for having,
while out hunting, killed his son, who carried on
a criminal intercourse with his step-mother; and
the reason alleged is, *quod latronis magis quam
patris jure eum interfecisset;* NAM PATRIA POTES-
TAS IN PIETATE DEBET, NON ATROCITATE, CONSIS-
TERE (*f*). But it deserves notice that in the
same part of the Digest where this passage occurs, a definition is given of those who came

(*c*) Dion. Hal. ii. 27.

(*d*) Dig. xxviii. ii. 11. Cic. pro Domo. §§ 29. 32. Sallust
mentions, without remark, an instance of the exercise of this
power. *Fuere extra conjurationem complures, qui ad Catilinam
initio profecti sunt. In his erat Fulvius, Senatoris F., quem retrac-
tum ex itinere parens necari jussit.* Bell. Cat. c. 39.

(*e*) See his Opusculum, *De jure occidendi, vendendi et exponendi
liberos apud veteres Romanos.* He says, *Rigorem Juris veteris
videntur primum mores subegisse, deinde leges.* Ib. cap. 4. And see
also Noodt *De partus expositione et nece apud veteres;* and Heinecc.
Syntag. Antiq. Rom. Jur. i. tit. 9.

(*f*) Dig. xlviii. ix. 1.

within the meaning of the *lex Pompeia de parri-
cidiis*, which applied to persons who were guilty
of the murder of kinsmen, and almost every kind
of relationship is mentioned, except that of
children.   In his commentary on the law, Marcian points out that the *mother*, who murders her
son or daughter, and the grandfather who murders his grandchild, are within its scope and
purview, but he makes no allusion to the father (*g*).
The inference seems to be, that at the time when
Marcian wrote, the murder of a child by its
father was not considered a *parricidium*, as the
murder of a brother or sister or son-in-law, or
step-son was.   But by an edict of the Emperor
Constantine, such an act of the father was expressly made liable to the punishment affixed to
a *parricidium*.   The words are, *si quis parentis*
AUT FILII . . . . *fata properaverit* . . . . *pœna
parricidii puniatur* (*h*).   There can, however, be
no doubt that even before that period the severity
of what has been called by Latin writers the
patria majestas was much relaxed, and the father's
power seems to have become restricted in ordinary
cases to the use of moderate corporal chastise-
ment; but where the domestic offence was of a
graver nature, he had the right of fixing the
punishment, which was to be pronounced by a
Judge; although we are not to suppose that even

(*g*) Ib. tit. ix. § 1.
(*h*) Cod. ix. tit. 17.

in that case he could deprive his son or daughter of life (*i*).

§ 3. Towards the mother the Roman law enjoined upon children the duty of showing due reverence and respect, and punished any flagrant instance of the want of it (*k*); but beyond this it seems to have recognised no right or claim on her part. She was not in the eye of that law their natural guardian, even where the father died intestate, leaving them under age; nor could he legally appoint her their guardian by will (*l*). And, in conformity with our own law, the rule was that she had no right to appoint a testamentary guardian, although (unlike our law in this respect) the Roman law did not treat such an act as an absolute nullity, but allowed it to be confirmed after due investigation before the proper tribunal (*m*). We may, therefore, con-

(*i*) Cod. viii. tit. 46, § 3 ; ix. tit. 15. Heinecc. *ubi supra*. Even at a much earlier period when the power of the father was absolute, he was supposed to exercise it as a judge sitting in a domestic forum and after a formal investigation. For proofs, see Dion. Hal. iii. 22; viii. 79. Val. Max. v. 8. 2. Senec. de Clement. i. 14, 15.

(*k*) Cod. viii. tit. 47, § 4.

(*l*) Dig. xxvi. tit. ii. § 26; tit. iii. § 1 ; tit. iv. § 6.

(*m*) Dig. iii. tit. iii. § 2. In this respect the Roman law seems to have acted upon the principle, *factum valet quod fieri non debuit*, a principle of questionable propriety and repudiated by the English law. It is a maxim which prevails perhaps in no code more than in that of the Hindus. See Strange's Hindu Law, i. 87.

clude with certainty that no cases, such as are discussed in the following pages relative to the *father's* right, ever occurred in the Roman Courts, for his will was practically absolute, and no amount of cruelty, neglect of duty, or immorality on his part, affected in the slightest degree his claim to the custody of his children. It must be understood that this remark does not apply to *guardians,* for they might be removed for personal misconduct or ill treatment of the minor; and "in many respects, indeed, the Court of Chancery, in the exercise of its authority over infants, implicitly follows the very dictates of the Roman Code" (*n*).

§ 4. In France, by the Code Civil, the authority over infants—whose minority in both sexes there continues until the age of twenty-one—is given exclusively to the father during his life, and after his death the right of the mother accrues (*o*). But the father may appoint, by his will or declaration made before a magistrate or notary, a special adviser to act in conjunction with the mother, without whose concurrence she can perform no act of guardianship. If, however, his right of interference is specially limited, she may act by herself in matters beyond the scope of his authority. The mother is not bound to assume

(*n*) Story's Eq. Jur. § 1350.
(*o*) Code Civil, §§ 373. 389.

the office, but in case she declines doing so, she must fulfil its duties until she nominates a guardian. If she accepts it, and afterwards wishes to re-marry, it is her duty to summon the *conseil de famille*, who will decide whether she ought to be allowed to retain the guardianship. The *conseil de famille* consists of six relatives of the parents—three on the paternal and three on the maternal side—who reside within a certain specified distance of the place where the guardianship is exercised (*p*). If the widow neglects this formality she forfeits all right to the guardianship of her children, and her second husband will be responsible for any previous laches on her part as guardian. But if the *conseil de famille*, when duly summoned, continue her in the office, they are obliged to associate with her as co-guardian the second husband, who thereby becomes responsible for the proper performance of the duties in future.

§ 5. Mr. Chancellor Kent gives the following summary account of the law upon the subject of the custody of minor children as it exists in the United States, and he cites as his authorities the cases collected in the subjoined note (*q*), of which

(*p*) Ib. § 407.
(*q*) *Archer's Case*, 1 Ld. Raym. 673. *Rex* v. *Smith*, Stra. 982. *Rex* v. *Delaval*, 3 Burr. 1434. *Commonwealth* v. *Addicks*, 5 Binney, 520. The case of *M'Dowles*, 8 Johns. Rep. 328. *Commonwealth*

those that have been decided in our own courts
will be more fully discussed in the course of this
treatise.   He says (r):—

"The father may obtain the custody of his
children by the writ of *habeas corpus*, when they
are improperly detained from him; but the
Courts, both of law and equity, will investigate
the circumstances, and act according to sound
discretion, and will not always, and of course,
interfere upon *habeas corpus*, and take a child,
though under fourteen years of age, from the
possession of a third person, and deliver it over
to the father against the will of the child.   They
will consult the inclination of an infant, if it be
of a sufficiently mature age to judge for itself,
and even control the right of the father to the
possession and education of his child, when the
nature of the case appears to warrant it."   He
mentions also that by the *New York Revised
Statutes* (s) the Supreme Court is empowered to
award a *habeas corpus* on behalf of the wife when
the husband and wife live separate without being
divorced, and to dispose of the custody of the
minor children in sound discretion; and the
Chancellor or a Judge may, upon *habeas corpus*,

v. *Nutt*, 1 Brown's Penn. Rep. 143.   *Ozanne* v. *Delile*, 17 Martin's
Louis. Rep. 32.   *Matter of Woolstonecraft*, 4 Johns. Ch. Rep. 80.
Creuze v. *Hunter*, 2 Cox's Cases, 242.   *De Manneville* v. *De
Manneville*, 10 Ves. 52.
    (r) Commentaries, vol. ii. p. 194, 2nd edit.
    (s) Vol. ii. p. 148, 149.

recover and dispose of any child detained by the society of *Shakers*. And again, " in consequence of the obligation of the father to provide for the maintenance, and, in some qualified degree, for the education of his infant children, he is entitled to the custody of their persons, and to the value of their labour and services. There can be no doubt that this right in the father is perfect while the child is under the age of fourteen years; but as the father's guardianship, by nature, continues until the child has arrived to full age, and as he is entitled by statute to constitute a testamentary guardian of the person and estate of his children until the age of twenty-one, the inference would seem to be that he was, in contemplation of law, entitled to the custody of the persons, and to the value of the services and labour of his children during their minority. This is a principle assumed by the elementary writers, and in several of the judicial decisions" (*t*).

The same learned author also states that in America " the father, and on his death the mother, is generally entitled to the custody of the infant children, inasmuch as they are their natural protectors, for maintenance and education. But the Courts of Justice may, in their sound discretion, and when the morals or safety, or interest of the children strongly require it, withdraw the infants from the custody of the father

(*t*) Commentaries, vol. 2, 193.

or mother, and place the care and custody of them elsewhere. So the power allowed by law to the parent over the person of the child may be delegated to a tutor or instructor, the better to accomplish the purposes of education" (*u*).

This power of the father ceases on the arrival of the child at the age of majority, which has been variously established in different countries, but in the United States, as in England, it is fixed at the age of twenty-one.

If no testamentary disposition of the guardian-ship of the child is made by the father " the mother after the father's death is entitled to the guardianship of the person, and in some cases, of the estate of the infant, until it arrives at the age of fourteen, when it is of sufficient age to choose a guardian for itself. In New York, the mother is in that case, by statute, entitled to the guardian-ship of the estate" (*v*).

§ 6. The general rule of law in this country is, that the legal power over infant children belongs to the father and that during his life the mother has none. In the words of Blackstone (*w*), " a

<hr>

(*u*) Mr. Chancellor Kent cites the following authorities :—*Matter of Woolstonecraft*, 4 Johns. Ch. Rep. 80. *Commonwealth* v. *Addicks*, 5 Binney, 520. *United States* v. *Green*, 3 Mason, 482. *Case of Wellesley* v. *Duke of Beaufort*, 2 Russ. 1. *The State* v. *Smith*, 6 Greenleaf, 462.

(*v*) Commentaries, vol. ii. 206. New York Rev. Statutes, i. 718, § 5.

(*w*) Comm. vol. i. 453.

mother, *as such*, is entitled to no power, but only to reverence and respect." And irrespectively of the statute 2 & 3 Vict. c. 54, of which the provisions will be hereafter considered, the father has, at common law, a right to the exclusive custody of his child even at an age when it still requires nourishment from its mother's breast. As was said by Mr. Justice Patteson (*x*), "the law is perfectly clear as to the right of the father to the possession of his *legitimate* children of whatever age they may be." And by Mr. Justice Littledale (*y*), "it is the universal rule, with some exceptions, that the father is entitled to the custody of a young child even against the will of the mother. In case of there being no father, then the mother is the person next entitled to its custody" (*z*). What these exceptions are will be considered in the course of the work.

§ 7. It must be admitted that the application of this law which enforces with such jealous care the rights of the father, has often been extremely harsh. He might be a man of the most immoral character, and his conduct towards the mother such as to render it impossible for her, without all sacrifice of dignity and self-respect, to live with him; and

---

(*x*) *Ex parte M'Clellan*, 1 Dowl. P. C. 34.

(*y*) *Ex parte Glover*, 4 Dowl. P. C. 293.

(*z*) That is, supposing that no testamentary guardian has been appointed by the father. See *post*, Chap. VII.

yet, provided only that he was cautious enough not to bring his children into actual contact with pollution, and did not physically ill treat them, he had the entire control over and disposition of them, and might embitter the life of the mother by depriving her of the society of her offspring. And what untold suffering might she not be called upon to endure, in the mental struggle between the affection which prompted her to submit to insult and injury for their sake, and the desire to escape from such usage by abandoning her home! The Legislature has at last, after much difficulty and opposition, provided a partial remedy for this evil, and, as will be seen hereafter, Courts of Equity are now enabled to make regulations on the subject which take into account the feelings of the mother, and are more in unison with the dictates of humanity (a).

§ 8. But " although in general parents are intrusted with the custody of the persons and the education of their children, yet this is done upon the natural presumption, that the children will be properly taken care of, and will be brought up with a due education in literature, and morals, and religion; and that they will be treated with kindness and affection; but whenever this presumption is removed, whenever (for example) it

(a) Stat. 2 & 3 Vict. c. 54. *Post*, Chap. VIII.

is found, that a father is guilty of gross ill treatment or cruelty towards his infant children; or that he is in constant habits of drunkenness and blasphemy, or low and gross debauchery; or that he professes atheistical or irreligious principles; or that his domestic associations are such as tend to the corruption and contamination of his children; or that he otherwise acts in a manner injurious to the morals or interests of his children; in every such case the Court of Chancery will interfere, and deprive him of the custody of his children, and appoint a suitable person to act as guardian, and take care of them, and to superintend their education" (b).   And to use the words of Lord Hardwicke, L. C., the Court of Chancery " has a general right delegated by the Crown as *parens patriæ* to interfere in particular cases for the benefit of such as are incapable to protect themselves" (c).

§ 9. It is unnecessary to discuss the grounds and reasons upon which the jurisdiction of the Court of Chancery, to interfere and remove the persons of infant children from the custody of their parents, is founded.   It is sufficient here to say, that it is " a jurisdiction which seems indispensable to the sound morals, the good order,

---

(b) Story's Eq. Juris. § 1341.

(c) *Butler* v. *Freeman*, Ambler, 302.

and the just protection of a civilised society" (d);
and that it is now too firmly established to be
shaken or questioned. "The truth is, that in
the constitution of the government of England
all powers in the administration of justice, which
are necessary in themselves, are vested in the
Crown; and are so vested to be exercised by
those ministers of the Crown to whom the jurisdiction has usually been delegated. The present
jurisdiction must be taken to be delegated to the
Court of Chancery, whenever there is a suit
respecting property in that Court" (e).

§ 10. Nor will the Court of Chancery wait
until some misbehaviour has actually occurred
on the part of parents or guardians, if it has
reason to suspect that they are about to act
improperly:—in the words of Lord Macclesfield,
"preventing justice is better than punishing
justice." This *dictum* occurred in a case (f)
where a petition was presented by some near
and noble relatives of the Duke of Beaufort and

(d) The reader will find this subject examined at length by the
late Mr. Justice Story, with his usual learning and ability, in the
34th Chapter of his Equity Jurisprudence. The following cases
may be consulted. *Duke of Beaufort* v. *Berty*, 1 P. Wms. 703.
Whitfield v. *Hales*, 12 Ves. 492. *De Manneville* v. *De Manneville*, 10 Ves. 59. *Shelley* v. *Westbrooke*, Jac. 266. *Lyons* v.
Blenkin, Jac. 245. *Creuse* v. *Orby Hunter*, 2 Cox, 242. *Wellesley* v. *Duke of Beaufort*, 2 Russ. 20, 21 ; 2 Bligh, N. S. 128.
(e) Ib. § 1349.
(f) *Duke of Beaufort* v. *Perty*, 1 P. Wms. 703.

his brother, Lord Noel Somerset, both infants, praying that the latter, who had been placed by his guardians, appointed under the will of the late Duke, at Westminster School, might be removed to Eton. The Lord Chancellor said, that as the Court would interpose where the estate of a man was devised in trust, so would it *a fortiori* concern itself in the custody of a child being devised to a guardian, who was but a person intrusted in that case, since nothing could be of greater concern than the education of infants. But as no good reason was given for the application in this instance, the Court refused to make any order on the subject.

§ 11. Previously to the passing of the act 2 & 3 Vict. c. 54, the rule was, that the Court of Chancery would only interfere in the case of infants where they were possessed of or entitled to property. "If any one," said Lord Eldon, "will turn his mind attentively to the subject, he must see that this Court has not the means of acting, except where it has property to act upon" (*g*). And in conformity with this principle Mr. Justice Story remarks (*h*), "The Court of Chancery will appoint a suitable guardian to an infant where there is none other, or none other who will or can act, at least, where the infant has property;

(*g*) *Wellesley* v. *Duke of Beaufort*, 2 Russ. 21.
(*h*) Eq. Juris. § 1338.

for if the infant has no property, the Court will perhaps not interfere. It is not, however, from any want of jurisdiction that it will not interfere in such a case, but from the want of means to exercise its jurisdiction with effect; because the Court cannot take upon itself the maintenance of all the children in the kingdom. It can exercise this part of its jurisdiction usefully and practically only where it has the means of doing so; that is to say, by its having the means of applying property for the use and maintenance of the infant." These latter sentences are taken from the judgment pronounced by Lord Eldon in the celebrated case of *Wellesley* v. *Duke of Beaufort* (*i*).

Lord Hardwicke also, in the case of *Butler* v. *Freeman* (*k*), already quoted, while he asserted the right of the Court of Chancery in very general terms, added the important qualification, that there *must be a suit depending* relative to the infant or his estate to entitle the Court to this jurisdiction. The occasion on which these remarks were made, was where a minor of the age of eighteen years had been trepanned into an improper marriage, which took place at Antwerp; and, on the petition of the father, the Court ordered that his son should be restored to him, and committed the wife and her brother, who

(*i*) 2 Russ. 1.   (*k*) Ambler, 301. *Supra*, p. 13.

had been active in bringing about the marriage,
to the Fleet Prison.

§ 12. The same doctrine is implied in which
was said by Sir John Leach, V. C., in *Wright* v.
Naylor (*l*), where a mother had clandestinely
taken her infant son away from his guardians, and
secreted him, and a petition was presented by
them, praying that he might be delivered up to
them that they might have the management of
him. The infant was entitled to about 500*l*.
under the will of his father, and the court said,
" In respect of the administration of the property
of the infant, the court has jurisdiction over his
person. Let the order be made as prayed by the
petition." And in *Wellesley* v. *Wellesley* (*m*), in
the House of Lords, Lord Redesdale said, that
the Chancellor might *perhaps* have exercised the
jurisdiction to deprive a father of the custody of
his children independent of the cause which had
been instituted in the Court of Chancery; but as
incident to the cause he apprehended that there
could be no doubt of the right to exercise the
jurisdiction.

§ 13. The mode in which Courts of Common
Law interfere in questions relating to the custody
of infants is by writ of *habeas corpus*, which, " in
general, lies to bring up persons who are in cus-

(*l*) 5 Madd. 77.   (*m*) 2 Bligh, N. S. 137.

C

tody, and who are alleged not to be legally restrained of their liberty. When the court clearly perceives that they are illegally detained, it will discharge them" (*n*). This part of the subject will be discussed in a subsequent chapter.

(*n*) Per *Littledale*, J., in *Ex parte Glover*, 4 Dowl. P. C. 293.

CHAPTER II.

INTERFERENCE OF COURTS OF EQUITY IN QUESTIONS OF PARENTAL CUSTODY.

§ 14. In a preceding quotation from Mr. Justice Story, we have seen that he enumerates examples of the cases in which the Court of Chancery will interfere to prevent the abuse of parental authority; and the determination of that court to do so, where there is property belonging to the infant upon which it can exercise jurisdiction, has been constantly asserted. It was strongly expressed by Lord Thurlow in a case (a), where a petition was presented to the court, stating that the father's affairs were embarrassed, that he was an outlaw, and resided abroad, and that his son, an infant, was entitled in remainder to a very considerable estate, and praying that the father might be restrained from taking his son abroad, or improperly interfering with his education: the petition further stated, that the mother lived separate from her husband, and

(a) *Creuze* v. *Hunter*, 2 Bro. Ch. Ca. 499, n.; and see *Whitfield* v. *Hales*, 12 Ves. 492.

principally directed the education of her son.
The Lord Chancellor ordered that the father
should be restrained from interfering with the
management of his child, without the consent of
two persons nominated for the purpose; and with
reference · to an objection of counsel, that the
court had no such jurisdiction, he said, that he
knew there was such a notion, but he was of
opinion that that court had arms long enough to
reach such a case, and to prevent a father from
prejudicing the health or future prospects of the
child. He added, that, whenever a case was
brought before him he would act upon this
opinion. If the House of Lords thought diffe-
rently, they might control his judgment, but he
certainly would not allow the child to be sacri-
ficed to the views of the father.

§ 15. In *De Manneville* v. *De Manneville*, (b) an
application had been made to the Court of King's
Bench for a writ of *habeas corpus*, and this having
been unsuccessful (upon grounds which will be
hereafter considered), a petition on behalf of the
mother and infant, the latter of whom was then
eleven months old, was presented to the Court
of Chancery, and stated that the mother had
married a French emigrant, and her property,
amounting to 700*l.* a year, had been settled to

(b) 10 Ves. 52. See *post*, Chap. III.

her separate use for life: that differences arose between them, and soon after the birth of their first child, Mrs. De Manneville quitted his house with it, and went to the residence of a friend, leaving a note for her husband, to inform him where he might see the child, and that ultimately he took it away by force. The prayer of the petition was, that the defendant, her husband, might be ordered to produce in court the infant, and that it might be delivered to her, the mother; and in case the court should be of opinion that the infant ought not to be taken from the father, then that he might be restrained from carrying away, or removing the petitioners, or either of them, out of the jurisdiction. The Lord Chancellor, in delivering judgment, adverted to the fact, that here the wife had voluntarily withdrawn herself from the society of her husband. He said, " I must consider the wife at present as living under circumstances, under which the law will not permit her to live (c). A very material consideration then arises, whether the child is to be removed to the custody of the mother, not living with the father according to the obligation of the marriage contract, which I am bound to consider existing until I am told by better authority than affidavits, that it ought no longer to subsist."

(c) By this expression is meant that the husband might institute a suit in the Ecclesiastical Court against his wife for the restitution of conjugal rights.

The affidavits in support of the petition con-
tains charges against the husband of irreligion
and dangerous political principles. With reference to these Lord Eldon said, " As to the political
and religious principles of this gentleman there is
but an unsatisfactory account upon those topics
by the affidavits, if any consideration ought to be
called to them. But the view that I take of those
affidavits is, as they create more or less probability that he may be removed from this country,
and, therefore, that the child may be removed; if
it is to follow his person." And upon the state
of facts laid before the court, his Lordship added,
" Looking at the father's situation, and taking his
own representation as to his inclination with
regard to this child, upon the affidavits there is a
fair suspicion of real danger, that the child may
be removed out of this country, and then according to Lord Macclesfield's opinion in the *Shaftesbury case*, the court must act upon that suspicion. Some method must be taken to secure to
the court that the person of the child shall remain in this country." An order was therefore
pronounced, that the defendant and all other persons should be restrained from taking the child
out of the kingdom; and he was afterwards
ordered to go before the Master, and give security
not to remove the child out of the kingdom.

§ 16. We see, therefore, that Lord Eldon did
not consider this a case in which he ought to

deprive the father of the custody of his child, but he carefully guarded himself against the supposition that the conduct of a parent might not be such as to warrant this exercise of authority on the part of the court.   He said expressly that in determining such a question, attention must be paid to the way in which a child was likely to be brought up.   " Since I have sat here, I removed a child from its father upon considerations such as these.   The father was a person in constant habits of drunkenness and blasphemy, poisoning the mind of the infant, and I thought it not inconsistent with a due attention to parental authority so abused to call in the authority of the king as *parens patriæ*" (d).   And, on another occasion, the same learned Judge said, " It is certain that the court will interfere against the acts of a guardian, if acting in a manner inconsistent with his duty; and it is equally clear that the court will control a parent if acting in a manner which he should not" (e).

§ 17. Let us now consider some instances of interference by the Court of Chancery on account of the conduct or character of the father.

That which may be regarded as the leading authority upon the subject is the well-known case of *Wellesley* v. *The Duke of Beaufort* (f), which

(d) Ib. 61, 62.   (e) *Lyons* v. *Blenkin*, Jac. 253.
(f) 2 Russ. 1.

was finally decided in the House of Lords (*g*). There the father had married a lady of large fortune, and had by her three children, a daughter and two sons, who were entitled to considerable property under the marriage settlement. He went abroad to avoid his creditors, and while on the continent formed an adulterous connexion with a Mrs. Bligh, in consequence of which his wife separated herself from him, and returned to England, taking with her, by his permission, the three minor children. She commenced a suit in the Ecclesiastical Court for a divorce, but died soon afterwards, and on her death bed committed her children to the care of her sisters, with a request that they would not allow the father to get possession of them. A bill was then filed in the name of the infants by their next friend against the trustees of the settlement, praying the usual accounts, and that a proper person might be appointed to have the care of their persons during their minorities. The father in the meantime returned to England, and presented a petition, in which he prayed that the aunts of his children, in whose custody they were, might, on a day named, deliver over the infants to him. During all this period the adulterous intercourse between Mrs. Bligh and the father continued, and heavy damages had been recovered in an

(*g*) *Wellesley* v. *Wellesley*, 2 Bligh, N. S. 124.

action for *crim. con.* brought by the husband against the latter.

When the petition came on for hearing, affidavits and letters were read which made out against Mr. Wellesley, the father, a case of the most profligate and immoral conduct. It was alleged that he had treated his wife with unkindness; that he lived in undisguised adultery; that he encouraged his sons to swear, and caused even his daughter to repeat profane and indecent language. In a letter addressed by him to the tutor of his sons he said, "there are certain things which ought to be let alone; a man and his children ought to be allowed to go to the Devil their own way, if he pleases."

In the course of an elaborate judgment, Lord Chancellor Eldon cited, with approbation, the opinion of Lord Macclesfield, already quoted, where he said that "if he had a reasonable ground to believe that the children would not be properly treated he would interfere, upon the principle that *preventing justice* was preferable to *punishing justice.*"

Lord Eldon also said, "I am not called upon to say what would be the consequence of the mere act of adultery on the part of the father. I will give no opinion upon that, because it may be attended with so many circumstances, or it may be unattended with so many circumstances as quite to alter the character of a case. Nor is it

necessary that I should give an opinion upon the
subject of drunkenness, as there is no such imputation in this case. At the same time I have no
difficulty in saying, that if a father be living in
a state of habitual drunkenness, incapacitating
himself from taking care of his children's education, he is not to be looked upon as a man of such
reason and understanding as to enable him to discharge the duty of a parent, and if such a case
were to occur again, as it has occurred before,
the court would take care that the children
should not be under the control of a person so
debased himself, and so likely to injure them."

§ 18. In this case Lord Eldon thought the
facts connected with the adultery so gross that
he emphatically declared that he ought to be
hunted out of society, if he hesitated for a
moment to say that he would sooner forfeit his
life than permit the girl to go into the company
of such a woman, or into the care and protection
of a man who had the slightest connexion with
that woman. The result was that the Lord
Chancellor made an order referring it to the
Master to inquire to what person or persons
willing, *other than the father*, to undertake the
same, the custody of the infants should be committed, and restraining the father from removing
them from the custody in which they then were
without the permission of the court.

§ 19. Against this order an appeal was presented to the House of Lords (h); but the judgment of the Lord Chancellor was unanimously affirmed.

In delivering his opinion on that occasion Lord Redesdale put the following case: " A lady who had high expectations might marry a person of the lowest and most profligate description, and her son might, after her death, be entitled to great property, and might also be a peer, the father being a person of the most abandoned description, of the worst education, the most improper person to have any care or direction of the management of that son; and is the doctrine to be endured, that there does not exist in this country a jurisdiction to control the power of the father in such circumstances? I deny that the law ever considered that he has such a power; it has always considered it as a trust. Look at all the elementary writings on the subject; they say, that a father is entrusted with the care of the children; that he is entrusted with it for this reason, because it is supposed his natural affection would make him the most proper person to discharge the trust."

§ 20. In the above case there was every probability that the father would bring his infant

(h) *Wellesley* v. *Wellesley*, 2 Bligh, N. S. 124.

daughter into contact with his mistress; indeed, Lord Eldon assumes this in his judgment, although he certainly adds, that he would not allow the girl to be under the care and protection of her father, if he " had the slightest connection with that woman." But this latter proposition must be received with caution, for the courts of equity repudiate interference where the father, however immoral his conduct may be, has sufficient sense of decency not to bring his children into contact with the person with whom he has formed a vicious connection. And, as will be shown hereafter, precisely the same distinction is recognised and acted upon in the courts of common law.

The following case was in Equity (i).—A petition was presented by a mother and daughter (the latter being about fourteen years of age) praying that the daughter might be placed under the mother's care, she offering to maintain her at her own expense, or that the mother might have access to her daughter at all convenient times; and it appeared that the father was living in habitual adultery with another woman, on account of which the mother had obtained a divorce in the Ecclesiastical Courts. The Vice Chancellor (Sir J. Leach) said, " This court has nothing to do with the fact of the father's adultery, unless

(i) *Ball* v. *Ball*, 2 Sim. 35.

the father brings the child into contact with the
woman. All the cases on the subject go upon
that distinction, when adultery is the ground of a
petition for depriving the father of his common
law right over the custody of his children."

The counsel for the petitioners admitted that
there was no proof that the father had actually
brought his daughter into contact with his mistress, but they urged that at all events liberty of
access should be granted to the mother. It appeared on affidavits that the child formerly lived
with her mother, and was at times allowed to go
to her father; but on one occasion, the father,
without any communication with the mother,
detained his daughter, and sent her to a school,
and the mother was ignorant for a long time what
had become of her child, and when after great
difficulty she found out the school, the mistress
refused to allow her to see the child except in her
presence. It was further stated, that the child,
when living with her father, had no society except
that of a female servant of all work, and that the
father's conduct was so gross and violent towards
the mother when she went to him to inquire
after her daughter's residence, that it was dangerous for her to be in his presence. The question pointedly put under these circumstances on
behalf of the mother to the court was this:—" Is
a child of fourteen years to be deprived, by the
brutal conduct of the father, of the company,

advice, and protection of a mother, against whom
no imputation can be raised?"

The Vice Chancellor, however, while he admitted that in a moral point of view he knew of
no act more harsh or cruel than depriving the
mother of proper intercourse with her child, stated
that he felt bound to say that in this case there
did not appear to him to be sufficient to deprive
the father of his common-law right to the care
and custody of his child. He considered that the
question resolved itself into one of authorities,
and he knew no case which would authorize him,
upon the facts as they appeared, to make the
order sought in either alternative. And he
mentioned two cases of a similar nature (*k*), in
which Lord Eldon had refused petitions precisely
similar. The petition therefore was dismissed.

§ 21. It is to be observed, that here there was
no cause between the parties in court other than
the matter arising out of the petition itself; nor
does it appear that there was any property to
which the child was entitled, and upon which the
Court of Chancery could exercise its jurisdiction.
If this had been the case, perhaps on account of
the general conduct of the father the decision
might have been different, and the court might
have acted upon the intimation thrown out by

(*k*) *Smith* v. *Smith* and *Gallini* v. *Gallini* not elsewhere reported.

Lord Eldon, when he said, that he "apprehended
that the jurisdiction which he had upon a *habeas
corpus* was exactly the same as if it was before a
Judge, and that a Judge attended to nothing but
cruelty, or personal ill-usage to the child, as a
ground for taking it from its father. *But where
there was a cause in court there were many other
considerations*" (*l*).

§ 22. In a very recent case a petition was presented in the Court of the Vice Chancellor of
England by a mother, Mrs. Warde, praying that
the custody of her five minor children might be
given up to her, on the ground that their morals
were likely to be corrupted by remaining with
their father. It appeared that in consequence of
the immoral conduct of her husband she had obtained a decree for a divorce from him in the
Ecclesiastical Court, and alimony to the amount
of 1200*l*. a year was awarded, the property in
settlement at the marriage being very considerable. The case was heard before the Vice Chancellor in his private room, who decided against
the petition, and said, that the rule of the court
in matters of this kind, as laid down in various
cases, was, that personal misconduct on the part
of the father was not of itself sufficient to deprive
him of the custody of his children, which nature
and the law gave him. To support such an

(*l*) Note (*b*) to *Lyons* v. *Blenkin*, Jac. 254.

application it must be shewn that there had been
an attempt by the father to poison the minds of
his children, or, at any rate, that they were subjected to scenes calculated to undermine their
morals.   Nothing, however, had been proved in
evidence before him (the Vice Chancellor) further
than that the father had been guilty of conduct
highly immoral and justly to be reprehended; but
at the same time it must be borne in mind that
such misconduct of his had been carried on in so
secret a manner that his wife had only been
apprised of it a short time before coming to this
court.   Under these circumstances, as there was
no proof that the children had been improperly
brought up by the father, or that any of his irre-
gularities had been suffered to reach the children,
the Vice Chancellor thought that the rule of law
which prevented the court from interfering between father and children, where the moral delin-
quencies of the parent were concealed from the
children, must prevail, and he ordered the three
eldest children to be given up to the father.
At the same time he said, that he considered
the conduct of the mother to be irreproachable,
and directed that the two youngest children,
who were of tender age, should remain with her;
but with respect to the others, he considered
himself bound by the rule of law, which he
approved, and which said that a child should
not be deprived of a father's protection so long

as there existed no proof of its being liable to contamination by remaining with him (*m*).

The mother appealed against this order to the Lord Chancellor, and fresh affidavits were filed, which disclosed gross immoralities on the part of the father, and shewed that he was bringing up his children in a way calculated to demoralize them, especially the eldest, a girl ten years of age.

While this appeal was pending, Mrs. Warde presented a second petition, stating her belief that Mr. Warde intended to withdraw both himself and children out of the jurisdiction of the court, and praying for an order to prevent his taking such a step. The Lord Chancellor made an order upon this petition, restraining Mr. Warde from taking the children out of the country pending the other petition.

In giving final judgment, the Lord Chancellor said that since the decision of the court below, fresh evidence had been furnished of such a nature that he felt convinced that, if it had been before the Vice Chancellor at the time of giving his judgment, he would have come to a different conclusion. From the evidence as it now stood, it was plainly to be seen that the conduct of Mr. Warde, in the neighbourhood in which he resided, was of such an objectionable and notorious cha-

(*m*) This case is not reported, but the judgment of the Lord Chancellor was given Jan. 20th, 1849.

D

racter that no modest woman dared to approach him, and at the same time there was too good reason to suppose that he was living with a person of improper conduct. Mr. Warde's own statement respecting this woman was, that he hired her at Brighton in the menial capacity of servant, but that he had afterwards for her usefulness promoted her to the office of housekeeper. Now, it appeared from the affidavits that this person was the only companion of the eldest Miss Warde, and in fact that she regularly took her seat at the table with the family, and in addition, it was alleged that it was not an uncommon practice for Mr. Warde, his daughter, and this woman to be seen walking about the grounds, all three of them with cigars in their mouths. Now, the habit of smoking was at all times and by all persons bad enough, but it became truly disgusting when practised by a young lady of her station in life, who, it was stated, had a large store of cigars by her for her own use. From all these disclosures it was pretty plainly to be inferred that this person was not living with Mr. Warde in the capacity of either cook or housekeeper. It next became important to look to the evidence respecting the education of Miss Warde; now, although there were statements that she was under various masters to learn the ordinary accomplishments of young ladies, there was not a single allegation that her religious or moral education was looked after. On the other hand, observations of Mr. Warde had been deposed to with a view of proving that he was not a religious character, and, although he had undoubtedly denied the truth of such statements, still he had done it in such a way as to leave the question, whether the inference drawn from his words was not substantially correct, altogether untouched, and the court would be more inclined to put credence in the statements of Mrs. Warde and her brother than in those of Mr. Warde. With such evidence before him of the grossly immoral conduct of Mr. Warde, and taking into consideration the great probability that he was now carrying on an improper intercourse with this woman, who was the only person to give Miss Warde any moral or religious instruction, he (the Lord Chancellor) felt bound to declare that Mr. Warde was unfit to have the custody of his daughter, and that she must be given up to her mother. With respect to the question of the other two children, at present with their father, he was of opinion that it was at all times better that children should not be brought up separately. If, unfortunately, it became necessary that they should lose the protection of one of their parents, it was far better that all the children should be brought up together than that half should be educated to side with the father, and the other half with the mother. Without, therefore, ex-

pressing any opinion, whether the conduct of
Mr. Warde was such as to disentitle him to the
custody of his son, his Lordship said that he
should direct that all the three children should
be given up to Mrs. Warde or to some other
person appointed by her, upon the service of the
order.

§ 23. Whatever difficulty there may be in
defining the degree of latitude which will be
allowed to opinions in matters of religion, before
the Court of Chancery feels itself justified in
interfering to protect infants from the poison of
infidelity, it is quite certain that where a father
avows himself an atheist, or ridicules and blas-
phemes the Christian religion, he will be deemed
an unfit person to have the custody of his children, and will (if they have property upon which
the jurisdiction of the court can be exercised,)
be restrained from getting possession of or inter-
meddling with them.   With reference to such
a case, Lord Eldon said that he should not be
justified in delivering the children over to the
custody of a father who deemed it his duty to
recommend to them the adoption of conduct in
some of the most important relations of life as
moral and virtuous which the law considers as
immoral and vicious (n).

But on another occasion, where the father,

(n) *Shelley* v. *Westbrooke*, Jac. 266.

who claimed possession of his children, as against
their aunt, who detained them from him, was an
Unitarian, the same learned Judge granted the
application, and laid down the general rule to be
observed in such cases by saying, " with the religious tenets of either party I have nothing to do,
*except so far as the law of the country calls upon
me to look on some religious opinions as dangerous
to society*" (*o*).

§ 24. Let us next consider whether, even if
there be no ground for interference with paternal
control on account of immoral conduct on the
part of the father, there may not be other causes
or circumstances which will justify the Court of
Chancery in removing his minor children from
his custody.

And first, it may, I think, be laid down that
mere insolvency or poverty is not such a cause.
Although a provision should be made for infants
from a fund in which he is not entitled to par-
ticipate, and he is unable to support them
adequately out of his own means of livelihood,
yet he cannot *on that account only* be compelled
to part with the care and superintendence of his
children, in order that they may enjoy the bounty
of others (*p*). And it is reasonable that the law

(*o*) *Lyons* v. *Blenkin*, Jac. 256.
(*p*) *Kilpatrick* v. *Kilpatrick*, Reg. Lib. 1828, A. fo. 2106; Macpherson on Infants, Part 1, p. 142, 143.

should be so; for, as was said on one occasion by
Lord Chancellor King, " it cannot be conceived
that because another thinks fit to give a legacy,
though never so great, to my daughters, therefore
I am by that means to be deprived of a right
which naturally belongs to me—that of being
their guardian" (q). A father, against whose
character there is no imputation, seems to have
an undoubted right to exercise an option whether
he will or will not surrender the education and
custody of his child to others, in order to secure
for it certain pecuniary advantages. But a
bequest to the father, on condition that he will
allow his infant to be committed to the care of
trustees appointed under the will, which provides
a fund for its maintenance, will not, even if there
is no gift over, be held to be *in terrorem* only,
and he must renounce the legacy if he refuses
to comply with the condition, and insists upon
retaining the infant under his own care (r).

§ 25. Admitting however the general rule to be

(q) *Ex parte Hopkins*, 3 P. Wms. 152. If, however, an infant
is entitled to an estate, and the father enters upon it, and applies
the rents and profits to his own use, being himself in insolvent
circumstances and regardless of the interests of the infant, the
Court of Chancery will appoint not exactly a guardian, which
cannot be during the father's life, but a person to act as guardian
of the estate and person of the infant. *Ex parte Mountfort*, 15
Ves. 445.

(r) *Colston* v. *Morris*, Jac. 257, n. (11) ; and see *Potts* v. *Norton*, 2 P. Wms. 110, note.

as stated in the preceding part of the last section, there is an important exception to be noticed; namely, that the father will not be permitted in such a case first to encourage expectations in his children, by allowing them to receive maintenance and education for a time out of the fund provided for them, and afterwards turn round and deprive them of the *continuance* of those advantages, by asserting his paternal right to have the control and management of them himself. By his previous conduct he has given an implied, if not an express assent to their participation in the benefit of the pecuniary provision; that assent has been acted upon, and it is too late for him afterwards capriciously to withdraw it. He has, as it were, estopped himself from so doing, having, as was said on one occasion by Lord Hardwicke, "waived his parental right" (*s*).

By attention to this distinction we may reconcile various judicial dicta of Courts of Equity, which at first sight seem to conflict. For instance, that which has been already quoted of Lord King, and the following of Lord Eldon, that " it is always a delicate thing for the court to interfere against the parental authority; yet we know that the court will do it in cases where the parent is capriciously interfering in what is clearly for their benefit" (*t*); and, " will the

(*s*) *Blake* v. *Leigh*, Amb. 307.
(*t*) *Lyons* v. *Blenkin*, Jac. 262.

court permit a parent, who cannot educate his
child in a manner suitable to the property which
the child derives from the bounty of another, to
withhold from it the education to which it is
entitled?" (u)

§ 26. These expressions were used in a case
which clearly illustrates the principle upon
which the Court of Chancery acts, and the
judgment of Lord Eldon so fully explains the
distinction here pointed out, that it is given at
some length. It will be found to contain a summary of the law on this part of the subject. The
facts were these: A grandmother had by will
devised lands, and given legacies to her three
granddaughters, whose father was living, and
empowered her daughter, their aunt, to manage
the property during their minority, and pay
and apply such part thereof, as to her should
seem reasonable and proper, towards their maintenance and education. She also appointed her
their guardian (v) and executrix of the will.
It should be stated that the father had previously
committed the three children to the care of their
grandmother, the testatrix, and the expenses of
their education had been defrayed by her. After

(u) Ib. 254.
(v) This was done of course under a mistake of law; for no
guardian could be appointed while the father was alive, as Lord
Eldon notices in his judgment. Ib. 261. Nor indeed could a
grandmother, under any circumstances, appoint a legal guardian.

her death they continued to reside in the same manner under the care of their aunt, who subsequently married; but by the provisions of her marriage settlement reserved to herself the management of her nieces and their fortunes. About this time differences arose between her and their father, who filed a bill against her and her husband for accounts of the fortunes of the infants, insisting that they should be placed under his care, and that, as he was not of ability to maintain them, a proper sum should be allowed to him for that purpose. At this period the infants were of the ages of nineteen, fourteen, and twelve respectively, and their father was a dissenting minister of limited means, formerly a Baptist, but latterly an Unitarian. He had obtained a writ of *habeas corpus*, directed to the aunt and her husband, and when the argument on the return to the writ took place, Lord Eldon thought that the best mode of deciding the question would be to have a short petition presented;—at the same time saying that the jurisdiction in such cases was to be very carefully exercised. A petition was accordingly presented by the father, praying that the infants might be restored to him, and the result was that his application was refused. The Lord Chancellor, in delivering judgment, said—

" The view I have taken of the case is of this sort. Here is a fund provided for the maintenance and education of these children, and I think

I am properly warranted by authorities in asserting that if a testator thinks fit to provide a fund
for the maintenance and education of children
during their minorities, and at the end of that
period makes a further provision for them, and
the father permits their maintenance to be supplied
from that source, *allowing them to be brought up
with expectations founded upon a particular species
of maintenance and education*, which he himself
cannot afford to give them, he is not (unless I
greatly mistake the matter), according to the
principles of this court, at liberty to say that he
will take them from the course of education which
they have hitherto pursued, and that too at a
period approaching to maturity of age.   He is not
at liberty to say, I will alter the course of education of my children, by applying more scanty
means to the purpose, and I will not permit them
to have the benefit of that sort of maintenance
and education which they have hitherto had; and
in consequence of which their views in life are
very different from what they would have been
without it."

The Lord Chancellor afterwards added, " No-
body can doubt that *if I give a provision to your
child, it does not give me or any one else a right to
control your care of her; not at all;* but, on the
other hand, if when she is young I was to give
her a considerable maintenance during her in-
fancy, which you could not have supplied, and a

large fortune afterwards, and you, the father, permit her to take the advantage of that education, which could not have been afforded but through my gift, could you afterwards stop short and say, that she should no longer have that advantage ? Under such circumstances the court would inquire what was most for her benefit."

An application was afterwards made on the part of the father for a rehearing, which was granted, and the case was in part re-argued; but while it was still *sub judice* a motion was made on the part of the aunt to dismiss the bill, on the ground that the suit did not appear to be for the benefit of the infants.

This was refused by the court, and the case was not finally disposed of until the eldest of the infants had attained the age of twenty-one, and married.

Lord Eldon persisted in his refusal to remove the children from the custody of their aunt, and stated his reason as follows: " The circumstance that decides me about not removing the children is this, that although the testatrix could not impose the terms of appointing a guardian where the father was living, yet the father, by his consent, might enable the guardian to act, and by his consent it appears that he has enabled the guardian to act, and by such consent these children have, with very little interruption, continued under the care and guardianship of the aunt.

All their habits have been acquired under the
roof of their aunt—all their connections have
been formed under their aunt; and it appears to
me that the father has so far given his consent to
this course of education, as to preclude him from
saying that he shall now be permitted to break in
and introduce a new system of education, which
cannot be consistent with the system to which
they have been habituated, and where so much
depends upon the quantum of supply for the
purpose which the discretion of this lady may
lead her to apply, if the testatrix has left her
the discretion of regulating the means for their
education."

The learned Judge also said, " It therefore does
appear to me that the testatrix, by the benefits
she has given these children out of her property,
has purchased the power of educating them in
the way, and under the control and guardianship,
which she has pointed out, *and the parent has
consented to*, and I cannot help thinking that
unless this gentleman can bring before the court
some complaint on the ground of improper conduct, he must be taken to have given his consent
to the course of education which has been pursued."

§ 27. It is important to attend to the exact
words used by Lord Eldon in these passages, for
otherwise an erroneous view may be taken of the

rule which he there lays down.   It was the conduct of the father, in apparently acquiescing in
the terms of the bequest, and permitting his child
to be brought up conformably thereto, during
a period sufficiently long to induce and encourage
in its mind expectations of a considerable fortune, which was held to prevent him from afterwards depriving the infant of the designed
benefit.   On another occasion Lord Eldon said,
that "the court would not, in general, permit
the father to disappoint the expectations of his
children" (*w*).

§ 28.   And this seems to have been the principle which governed the opinion of Lord Thurlow
in the case of *Powell* v. *Cleaver* (*x*).   There an
uncle left by will to his nephew, a minor, whose
father was alive, property on the express condition that certain trustees named in the will
should have the care and guardianship of the
nephew during his minority.   The father allowed
his son to enjoy for some time the benefits of the
education provided for him by the trustees under
the uncle's will, but a dispute afterwards arose
whether the guardianship ought to be in the
father or the trustees of the will.   Lord Thurlow
said, " Lord Bathurst decided a case where there

(*w*) *Anon.* Jac. 254, n. (*b*), and see *Potts* v. *Norton*, 2 P. Wms.
110, n.   *Blake* v. *Leigh*, Amb. 306.
   (*x*) 2 Bro. Ch. Ca. 499.

was a Roman Catholic father, to whose son there was an estate given by a Protestant. It is no where laid down that the guardianship of a child can be wantonly disposed of by a third person. The wisdom would be not to raise points on such a question, as the court will take care that the child shall be properly educated for his expectations. It must be laid before the court how the son is now disposed of." Upon this point, however, nothing further occurs in the report of the case.

§ 29. In the two following cases there does not appear to have been any consent on the part of the father, beyond what might be implied from the fact of his previous non-interference. The court, however, would not allow him, being without any ostensible means of support to deprive his infant children of the benefit of proper maintenance and education by taking possession of them himself. A man had been outlawed and was living abroad in very embarrassed circumstances, but on his return to this country, was about to remove his son, who was eleven years of age, from the school where he had been placed by his mother, and carry him abroad (z). The mother presented a petition to the Court of Chancery to prevent this being done. And upon the undertaking of cer-

(z) *Creuze* v. *Hunter*, 2 Cox, 242 ; 2 Bro. Ch. Ca. 500, n.; Reg. Lib. A. 1789, fo. 456 ; Jac. 250.

tain parties approved of by the court that they would provide for and superintend the infant's education, it was ordered that he should be placed under their care, and that the father should be restrained from removing his son from the school and situation in which he was then placed, and from carrying him abroad out of the jurisdiction of the court, and from using or employing any means for that purpose.

A decision similar in effect to this was pronounced by the Commissioners of the Great Seal in 1792 (a). A petition had been presented by four infants and their mother, praying that it might be referred to one of the Masters to approve of a proper person to have the care of their persons and superintendence of their education during the minority of the former, and that the father might be restrained from removing them from the schools and situations where they were then placed. It appeared that the father had become bankrupt, and a legacy of 2000l. having been left to the wife, the assignees proposed that 1000l. should be paid to them, and the residue settled to the separate use of the wife for her life, and after her decease in trust for the children. Affidavits were also sworn, which stated, that the father, by his cruel behaviour to his wife, had compelled her to exhibit articles of the peace against him. He had not any settled

(a) *Ex parte Warner*, 4 Bro. Ch. Ca. 101.

place of abode, and was wholly unable to provide for his family; and he threatened to remove
his children from the schools where they had been
placed by their mother and her relatives, and take
them into his own custody. It was also alleged
that he was a very unfit and improper person to
have the care and management of his children.
Upon these facts the court decreed, that an order
should issue as prayed by the petition.

§ 30. It is to be observed, however, that in
both these instances there were other circumstances beyond the mere facts of the father's insolvency and previous non-interference, which
may have influenced the court in its decision.
In the one case the father had been outlawed, and
was about to carry his infant son abroad out of
the jurisdiction, an act which the Court of Chancery has always most properly viewed with great
jealousy and disfavour, as will be more fully
shown hereafter. In the other, there was an
allegation that the father was a very unfit and
improper person to have the care and management of his children. How far this may have
weighed with the court does not appear, but it
would be unsafe to conclude that had there not
been these additional facts, unfavourable to the
claim of the father in either case, his right to the
custody of his children would have been interfered
with.

§ 31. But although acquiescence on the part of the father, whereby his children have been enabled for a time to enjoy the benefits of the bounty of others, is thus held to operate as a kind of estoppel, and prevent him from depriving them of those benefits, yet it seems that a mere prospective engagement on his part to allow his children to live apart from him under certain circumstances, will not be binding upon him. Thus in the case of husband and wife, where a deed had been executed, whereby the former had covenanted, in the event of a separation between them, to permit their children to reside with the latter, and to be educated under her care and superintendence, the Court of Chancery, upon a return made to a writ of *habeas corpus*, which had been issued on the petition of the father, ordered that the infants should be delivered up to him, although the contemplated separation had taken place, and the infants were of tender years, the one being five years, and the other only seven months old (*b*).

The nature also of the provision made for the infants must be taken into account. To use the words of Lord Eldon, there have been in all such cases of interference solid considerations, and not merely expectations. There has been some immediate irrevocable provision, by which the child could be brought up in a manner suitable to its

(*b*) *Earl and Countess of Westmeath*, Jac. 251, n. (*c*).

E

future property. The court has then said, that it would not permit the father wantonly and capriciously to deprive the child of that benefit.

The occasion on which these remarks were made was where a petition had been presented to the Court of Chancery by the mother of some infants, who was living apart from her husband, and was possessed of considerable property, settled to her separate use (c). The income of the husband was small, and the prayer of the petition was that the infants might be placed with her, or that it might be referred to the Master to approve of a plan for their education, and to appoint a proper person to have the care of them, the mother offering to provide for their maintenance out of her separate income. She also prayed that the father might be restrained from taking them out of the jurisdiction. It was urged, in support of the petition, that the father's income was not sufficient to enable him to give the infants an education suitable to their condition in life and to their expectations, and that it would therefore be for their benefit that their mother's proposal should be granted. The Lord Chancellor, however, refused the application, on the ground that the provision mentioned was a mere offer; but he added, that his decision was without prejudice to any other application or proposal which might be made in case of any permanent provision

(c) *Anon.* cited Jac. 264, n. (a).

being made for the infants. Moreover, as they
were wards of the Court, the father must be restrained from taking them abroad, or depriving
the mother of such access to her children as was
necessary to keep alive in them feelings of
obedience and affection towards her.

The father afterwards received an appointment
abroad, which required him to be absent from
this country for several years, and he petitioned
the court for leave to take the infants with him.
He stated that he was desirous of being reconciled
to his wife, and it appeared that he had with that
view made some overtures to her which she had
declined; and his Lordship ultimately ordered that
the father should be at liberty to take the infants
abroad with him, undertaking to bring them, or
such of them as should be living, back with him;
and he was half-yearly to transmit, properly
vouched, to be laid before the court the plan of
tuition and education for each of the infants,
actually adopted and in practice at the time of
such half-yearly returns, specifying particularly
where and with whom they resided.

§ 32. Where the father was dead and the
mother resided abroad, and a large sum of money
was settled upon their infant daughter, upon
condition that she should remain under the care
of the settlor, or of such person as he should
approve, until she attained the age of twenty-one,

it was referred to the Master to consider whether it would be proper to appoint the settlor to be guardian of the infant, taking into consideration the effect of the settlement (*d*).

§ 33. The general result of the authorities cited and commented upon in the present chapter seems to be this: the Court of Chancery will, where there is property on which it can exercise an effectual jurisdiction, interfere to prevent the abuse of parental authority, and to protect the interests both moral and pecuniary of infants. It will for that purpose deprive a parent of the custody of his child, if he pollutes its mind by bringing it into the presence of and contact with vice. But although in one sense, if his conduct is immoral, he may be said to do this whenever he associates with the infant himself, something more is meant by the terms *presence and contact*. They imply that the child is allowed to live with or visit the paramour of the parent. The court will also interfere, where a father treats his child with cruelty, or is given to habits of gross drunkenness, or professes atheism, or educates it in principles destructive of morality and the well being of society—but not where his opinions are merely those of some recognised form of dissent. Furthermore, if property be settled upon an infant, upon condition that the father surrenders

(*d*) *Fagnani* v. *Selwyn*, Jac. 263.

his right to the custody of its person, and he by acquiescing for a time and permitting the child to be educated in a manner conformably to the terms of the gift or bequest, encourages in it corresponding expectations, he will not be allowed to disappoint them by claiming possession of the infant.

It must be borne in mind however, that by stat. 2 & 3 Vict. c. 54, which will be considered in a separate chapter, a larger discretion is now vested in the Court of Chancery, with respect to the claims *of the mother*, than was deemed to be within its power when the cases were decided which have been here discussed.

CHAPTER III.

INTERFERENCE OF COURTS OF COMMON LAW BY
WRIT OF HABEAS CORPUS.

§ 34. IN Courts of Common Law the question
of custody arises chiefly on returns to writs of
habeas corpus, which are directed to parties, who
have possessed themselves (improperly, as it is
alleged) of the persons of infants, and who are
called upon to show cause why they detain
them (*a*). And the production in court of a
letter from a daughter to her mother, who was
separated from her husband, in which the daughter
complained that she was kept by her father in
his house, and by him severely used, has been
deemed sufficient to justify the grant of a *habeas
corpus*, returnable immediately, to compel the

(*a*) "On a writ of *habeas corpus* being applied for by the father
to have the children restored to him in the Court of King's Bench,
that court inquires whether they are wards of the Court of Chancery, and whether there are any proceedings in that court respecting them. If the Court of King's Bench finds there are such
proceedings it declines to grant the writ." Per Lord *Manners*, in
Wellesley v. *Wellesley*, (Dom. Proc.) 2 Bligh, N. S. 142. See *R.*
v. *Isley*, 5 Ad. & Ell. 441. *Post*, section 43.

father to produce his daughter in court in order
that she might be examined (b).

§ 35. The distinction between the powers of a
Court of Common Law and those of a Court of
Equity in this matter is pointed out by Lord
Redesdale in the following passage (c):—

"The care of the person to protect from
violence belongs to the Court of King's Bench,
but the care of the person with respect to education does not belong to the Court of King's Bench,
and the Court of King's Bench disclaims any such
right: therefore as to the care and protection for
the purpose of education, it belongs to this Court
(of Chancery) which has exercised the jurisdiction." The same view of the matter was taken
in *Ex parte Skinner* (d), in the Common Pleas,
by Best, C. J., who said, "in cases of similar
applications to the Court of King's Bench, they
generally refer the parties to a Master in Chancery, who may ascertain whether there is suffi-

(b) *Archer's case*, 1 Ld. Raym. 673. The report designates the
daughter as *Mrs.* Eleanor Archer, which might convey the idea
that she was a married woman; but it is well known that at that
period (the reign of Wm. 3), it was common for unmarried ladies
to be addressed with that prefix to their names. No mention is
made in the report of an affidavit in this case, and in a note, Holt,
C. J. is stated to have said "without doubt a *habeas corpus* may
be granted upon the sight of a letter." But at the present day
it seems that an affidavit would be required.

(c) *Wellesley* v. *Wellesley* (Dom. Proc.), 2 Bligh, N. S. 136.

(d) 9 Moore, 278.

cient property to provide for the support of the
child or whether it might be made a ward of that
court, or he might appoint a guardian to take
care of it; and that therefore appears to me to
be the wisest and proper course; at all events,
our authority can only be co-equal with that of
the Court of King's Bench. But the Court of
Chancery has a jurisdiction as representing the
king as *parens patriæ*, and that court may accordingly, under circumstances, control the right
of a father to the possession of his child, and
appoint a proper person to watch over its morals
and see that it receives a proper education; and
if a sum equivalent to its maintenance can be
obtained, the Lord Chancellor will order it to be
done without inquiring where the funds are to
come from."

Lord Eldon also observed in an anonymous
case, which was privately heard before him (*e*),
that where the infant was a ward of the court,
there were many circumstances to which he could
give attention which could not weigh with him
on a *habeas corpus* alone, without any cause in
court. He said also, that he apprehended that
the jurisdiction which he had upon a *habeas
corpus* was exactly the same as if it was before a
Judge (*i. e.* a common law Judge) (*f*), and that

(*e*) Reported Jac. 254.
(*f*) On this point, see *Crowley's case*, 2 Swanst. 1; Com. Dig.
Habeas Corpus (A), and Stat. 31 Car. 2, c. 2, § 2, 3.

a Judge attended to nothing but cruelty or personal ill usage to the child, as a ground for taking it from its father.   But where there was a cause in court there were many other considerations to be attended to, as in the case then under discussion, where an aunt of the children had made an appointment in their favour, which she would not continue if they resided with their father. The Lord Chancellor proceeded to say, that he could not attend to that circumstance on a writ of *habeas corpus*, but in a cause it might have some weight.

§ 36.   We see that Lord Eldon here states that a Judge at common law, in considering the question, whether an infant shall be taken from the custody of its father or not, does not attend to anything as a ground for such removal except cruelty or personal ill usage to the child.   But we shall find that this is too limited a rule, unless we give the words " cruelty or personal ill usage" a wider sense than that which they usually bear, and make them embrace cases of moral contamination; for a well founded apprehension that a female infant, for instance, will by residence with its father be exposed to moral pollution, is sufficient to deprive him, at common law, of the right to the custody of his child.   The proof of this will sufficiently appear as we proceed.

§ 37. The rule that prevails in cases where the writ of *habeas corpus* is applied for was stated by Lord Mansfield to be as follows (*g*): "The court is bound *ex debito justitiæ*, to set the infants free from an improper restraint; but they are not bound to deliver them over to any body, nor to give them any privilege." Here we see it laid down that the delivery of an infant into the custody of any party is discretionary with the court, although it is bound to release it from an improper custody. In other words, that the court feels itself compelled to act so far as to determine what is an improper custody, and to relieve against it; but not to go further, and select a *custos* or guardian for the child. It will, however, be shown hereafter, that in later times a different view has been taken by our common law Judges of their obligations in this matter, and they have not deemed themselves restricted to so imperfect an exercise of authority, as merely to set the infant free from improper restraint, without determining into whose hands its custody ought to be committed (*h*).

§ 38. The facts of the case, in which Lord Mansfield laid down the above cited rule were these (*i*):—Ann Catley (the daughter of a coach-

(*g*) *R.* v. *Delaval*, 3 Burr. 1436.
(*h*) *R.* v. *Isley*, 5 Ad. & Ell. 441. See *post*, section 43.
(*i*) 3 Burr. 1434; 1 W. Bl. 409, S. C.

man) was apprenticed by her father, at the age of sixteen years, to Bates, a music master, for seven years.   When she was about nineteen years old, she formed a criminal connection with Sir Francis Delaval, and as Bates threatened to turn her out of doors, Sir Francis took a lodging for her mother, and furnished it, the music master allowing her 25*l.* a-year for her board, and it being agreed that he should have her earnings as a public singer. Afterwards Sir Francis obtained a general release from Bates to the girl, and her father and she agreed that she should bind herself apprentice to Sir Francis for the residue of the seven years, and he covenanted to instruct, or cause her to be instructed, in the art of music.   The father, however, applied to the court for a criminal information against Delaval, Bates, and the attorney employed to prepare the last-mentioned indenture, for a conspiracy to debauch his daughter, and also for a *habeas corpus* directed to Delaval to bring up the body of the infant.   This the latter did, and the court discharged the girl out of his custody.   Her father then attempted to seize her in court, but was not permitted, and he was reprimanded by Lord Mansfield for the contempt.   Ann Catley then declared her attachment to Sir Francis, and her unwillingness to go home with her father, upon which the Solicitor General applied to the court to protect her from any violence *redeundo*.   But as it was plain that she intended to continue her cohabitation with her seducer, the Court hesitated and said, that *such protections depended upon the circumstances of the case.*   " Sometimes we go so far as to send an officer with the parties home (*k*), at other times we only protect in the face of the court. It may or may not be proper for a father to have the custody of his child under age, till arrived at years of discretion.   In the present case he seems to have assigned over his parental authority to Bates, the master, by the indenture of apprentice-ship " (*l*).   It was then ordered that cause should be shown on a subsequent day against the infor-mation, and that in the meantime no person should molest the girl on pain of being committed.

When cause was shown, it appeared that the conduct of the minor was so thoroughly vicious that the court declared they had no hopes of reclaiming her, and the only question was, whether any temporal crime had been committed deserving the interposition of the court.   They thought that both the father and mother were originally parties to the ruin of their daughter, although now the former appeared as the prose-cutor of the information.

(*k*) See *R.* v. *Clarkson,* 1 Strange, 445.
(*l*) Compare *Ex parte Earl of Westmeath,* Jac. 251, note (*c*), and *R.* v. *Mead,* 1 Burr. 542.   *R.* v. *Winton,* 5 T. R. 89.

The result was, that they refused actively to interfere, and Lord Mansfield said, " In the present case, upon the circumstances, we think it very improper for her to go to her father.   He used her ill before she was apprenticed, and by the indenture has parted with all his parental authority (*m*).   She must be discharged, and of course will have her privilege *redeundo*; but I will not interpose in any extraordinary manner."

This decision seems to have proceeded upon two grounds: first, the vicious propensities of the daughter, and, secondly, the depraved conduct of the father.   On account of the former, the court had no hopes that by changing the custody the girl would be reclaimed, and the father had disentitled himself to any remedy at the hands of the court by having been a party to his daughter's dishonour.

§ 39. The right of the father was strongly asserted by the Court of King's Bench in the case of *R.* v. *De Manneville* (*n*), (which afterwards came before the Court of Chancery, as has been previously noticed) (*o*), and it must be admitted that it presents some features of peculiar hardship.   The affidavit upon which a writ of *habeas corpus* directed to the defendant to bring up the

(*m*) As to the question of emancipation of infants for the purposes of settlement under the Poor Law, see *R.* v. *Inhabitants of Scammonden*, 8 Q. B. 349.

(*n*) 5 East, 221.   (*o*) *Supra*, p. 20.

body of an infant, his daughter eight months
old, was obtained, stated, that he was a French-
man, and had married the mother of the child,
an Englishwoman, by whom he had this only
child. That she, not long after their marriage,
had separated herself from him, on account, as
she alleged, of ill treatment, and kept the child
whom she was nursing with her. That in the
night time the defendant found means, by force
and stratagem, to get into the house where she
was, and had forcibly taken the child then at the
breast, and carried it away almost naked in an
open carriage in inclement weather, with a view,
as the mother apprehended, of taking it out of
the kingdom. This last allegation, however,
with respect to taking the child abroad, was
proved to rest on no sufficient foundation.
There were affidavits contradicting the other
statements, but the court would not allow them
to be read, and Lord Ellenborough, C. J.,
observed, that as the ground of removal out of
the kingdom was done away, it lay on those who
applied for the writ to show that the father was
not entitled to the custody of the child. Afterwards, in delivering judgment, the Lord Chief
Justice said, " We draw no inferences to the dis-
advantage of the father. But he is the person
entitled by law to the custody of his child. If
he abuse that right to the detriment of the child,
the court will protect the child; but there is no

pretence that the child has been injured for want
of nurture, or in any other respect. Then he
having a legal right to the custody of his child,
and not having abused that right, is entitled to
have it restored to him."

In the course of argument reference was
made to *Litton's case*, which came before the
court in 1781, on an application for a *habeas
corpus* by the mother to bring up the body of a
child who had been placed at school, from whence
it had been taken by its father. There had been
articles of separation, by which the father had
bound himself to let the mother have access to
the child, and Lord Mansfield said, that the
court could not at any age take a child from the
father; but that as he had constrained himself,
by the articles to let the mother have access (*p*),
if he chose to take the child home, he must provide for the access of the mother to it there.

In *R.* v. *De Manneville*, Lawrence, J., mentioned that since *Lytton's case*, an application of
the same sort had been made by Sir W. Murray
to obtain possession of a child of five years old,
which the mother kept from him. There Lord
Kenyon had no doubt but that the father was
entitled to have the custody of the infant, unless
the court saw reason to believe that he intended
to abuse his right by sacrificing the child, which
was suggested to be his motive for getting pos-

(*p*) See *Ex parte Earl of Westmeath*, Jac. 251, n. (*c*).

session of it.   Sir W. Murray had been divorced
from the mother, and there was not, as it was
alleged, any reason to think that the child was
his, though born before the divorce.   But the
court did not think that a sufficient ground to
deny him the custody of it.

§ 40. In *Blisset's case* (*q*), which came before
Lord Mansfield, a writ of *habeas corpus* had been
obtained by the father to recover possession of
his female child, who was about six years old,
and resided with her mother.   The latter at the
time was living separate from her husband, on
account of his ill treatment of her (*r*); and it
was alleged that the child was likely to receive
an improper education from her father, and was
not well used by him.   He had also become a
bankrupt.   Lord Mansfield said, " If the parties
are disagreed, the court will do what shall appear
best for the child; fix on a boarding school, and
the court will have no objection; let the child in
the mean time stay, so that the rule may be
made with the concurrence of the family.   The
natural right is with the father; but if the father
is a bankrupt, if he contributed nothing for the
child or family, and if he be improper, for such
conduct as was suggested at the Judge's

(*q*) Lofft. 748.
(*r*) See the observations of Lord Eldon, in *De Manneville v. De Manneville*, 10 Ves. 59. *Supra*, p. 21.

Chambers, the court will not think it right that the child should be with him."

But it is necessary to call attention to the observations of Patteson, J., upon this case. In *Ex parte McClellan* (*s*), that learned Judge said, "That case (*i. e. Blisset's*) was doubted a great deal by the Court of Common Pleas in the case of *Ex parte Skinner* (*t*), an infant, in which the court doubted its authority so to interfere." The report, however, of *Ex parte Skinner*, does not state any expression of doubt on the part of the court as to the authority of *Blisset's case.* The exact words there used by Best, C. J., were the following, and they contain the only allusion that was made to the decision of Lord Mansfield:—"I was referred to *Blisset's case*, and it certainly is extremely strong to show, that the power of assigning the custody of a child brought before the Court of King's Bench was discretionary, if the father appeared to be an improper person to take it; and I therefore thought that the most prudent course would be to assign it over to the care of a third person, and which was acceded to by both its parents. But it now appears that the father has removed the child, and has the custody of it himself; and no authority has been cited to show that this court has jurisdiction to take it out of such custody for the purpose of delivering it over to the mother."

(*s*) 1 Dowl. P. C. 85.   (*t*) 9 Moore, 278.

F

The distinction therefore that seems to be here
taken is this: so long as the infant is not in the
custody of its father, the court will, under certain circumstances, prevent him from obtaining
possession of it; but if he has already got possession of the child, the court will not interfere to
take it from him, at least unless there be apprehension of ill treatment or moral contamination
by him.

§ 41. In some cases, even where in a moral
point of view, the conduct of a father has been
very unfavourable to his right to the custody of
his children, it has been notwithstanding upheld.
Thus, in *R.* v. *Greenhill* (*u*), the mother had
separated herself from her husband on account
of the open and avowed adultery of the latter
with another woman; and she had taken away
with her her three children, females, aged respectively five years and a half, four and a half,
and two and a half, to the house of their
maternal grandmother, where they were residing
at the time when Mr. Greenhill obtained a writ
of *habeas corpus*, commanding his wife to produce
the bodies of his three children before Patteson,
J., at his house. It was stated on affidavits,
and not denied by Mr. Greenhill, that when he
obtained the writ he was living under a feigned

(*u*) 4 Ad. & Ell. 624; and see *In re Pulbrook*, 11 Jur. 185.
In re Fynn, 12 Jur. 713, and note at p. 720.

name with a woman who passed as his wife at a
lodging in London, and that he acknowledged
that the adultery was still continuing. It was
also stated that he could at any time have, and
had, in fact, had, access to the children where
they then were. The grandmother deposed, that
if the children were placed with their father
there was great probability that they would be
brought into contact with a female of an abandoned and profligate character. Mr. Justice
Patteson, after taking time for consideration,
ordered that the children should be delivered up
to their father. The order was made a rule of
court, but Mrs. Greenhill refused to give up the
children, and a rule *nisi* was obtained for an
attachment against her, for a contempt. She,
however, in the same term, obtained a rule *nisi*,
calling upon Mr. Greenhill to show cause why
the order of Patteson, J., should not be set aside,
and the rule, making it a rule of court, discharged. The matter thus came before the
court. It should be mentioned also, that Mrs.
Greenhill had already instituted proceedings
(which were then depending) in the Ecclesiastical
Court for a divorce and alimony.

Affidavits were put in on behalf of Mr. Greenhill, in which he stated that he had offered, if his
wife would forgive him, to live with her wher-
ever she wished, and to give up his adulterous
connection, but without success; that the children,

if taken out of his custody, would lose materially
by family arrangements, which, to his knowledge
and belief, would essentially affect their future
interests; that his wife had no means of supporting them; that the children, if separated
from him, would, as he believed, be brought up
in detestation of him, and that his mother was a
very proper person to be entrusted with them;
that he never contemplated for a moment depriving his wife of the privilege she had as a
mother of seeing her children, and had repeatedly
expressed himself to her to that effect; that he
had never taken either of his children near to his
mistress's residence, or his mistress to his own
house, or any other place where his wife or
children were, nor had he entertained the thought
of bringing his wife or children in contact with
her. It was afterwards sworn by Mr. Greenhill
that he believed that Mrs. Greenhill had taken
the children with her out of the kingdom.

On the part of the mother it was said, that she
was willing to abide by any direction of the court
which might leave her access to her children.
Upon this Lord Denman, C. J. remarked, " The
children are not in court; nor have we any certainty that the order we might make would be
complied with."

The court ultimately discharged the rule obtained by Mrs. Greenhill, and thus decided that
the father was entitled to the custody of the

children.   Lord Denman said, "There is in the first place, no doubt, that when a father has the custody of his children, he is not to be deprived of it except under particular circumstances; and those do not occur in this case; for, although misconduct is imputed to Mr. Greenhill, there is nothing proved against him which has ever been held sufficient ground for removing children from their father : here it is impossible to say that such danger exists.   Although there is an illicit connexion between Mr. Greenhill and Mrs. Graham, *it is not pretended that she is keeping the house to which the children are to be brought* (v), or that there is anything in the conduct of the parties so offensive to decency as to render it improper that the children should be left under the control of their father.   And he promises the same conduct with respect to them for the future.   The present rule was not granted because the court entertained much doubt, but from a desire to avoid increasing the misfortunes of this family" (w).

(v) See, however, *Ex parte Skinner*, 9 Moore, 278, where the affidavits stated that the infant, six years of age, was living with the mistress of the father, and that "she took the child to him every day;" and yet the court decided that they had no authority to interfere, "and more particularly so, as there was no charge of ill treatment by the father." Ib. 282. But *quære*, whether the law would be so laid down now ?

(w) During the debate in the House of Lords (July 18th, 1839) on the Custody of Infants' Bill, Lord Denman, C. J. said, "In the case of *The King* v. *Greenhill*, which had been decided in 1836, before himself and the rest of the Judges of the Court of King's Bench, he believed that there was not one Judge who had not felt

§ 42. In the course of the argument in this case, *R.* v. *Dobbyn* (*x*), was cited on behalf of the mother. But the proceedings there terminated in an agreement between the parents who disputed the possession of their child, to abide by the decision of a barrister appointed by the court. It is, however, so far important, as it shows that it is not sufficient for the father merely to establish his strict legal right, where there is such conduct on his part as imperils the morals of his child. The reasons alleged by the wife for not giving up her daughter, who was aged six years, to the care of the father were, that his time was principally devoted to the gaming-table, and the society of women of infamous character; that he was of a brutal disposition, and had attempted the life of his wife, desiring the woman with whom he lived to turn her out of doors, and declaring that she was not his wife but his discarded mistress.

The way in which the matter came before the court was, by the refusal of the wife to make any return to a writ of *habeas corpus*. She was ac-

---

ashamed of the state of the law, and that it was such as to render it odious in the eyes of the country. The effect in that case was, to enable the father to take his children from his young and blameless wife, and place them in the charge of a woman with whom he cohabited." See Hansard's Parl. Deb. vol. 49, (3rd series), p. 493. But according to the report of the case, the court thought that there was no evidence that the children were likely to be brought into contact with the father's mistress. If the fact had been so, the decision would probably have been very different.

(*x*) See note (*a*) to *R.* v. *Greenhill*, 4 Ad. & Ell. 644.

cordingly arrested, and was asked by the court whether she would undertake to appear before a Judge at Chambers, and bring her daughter with her: but this she declined to do. She was then examined upon interrogatories, and reported in contempt. By consent, the sentence was postponed until the following term, and in the meantime, the result was as above mentioned. We may not unreasonably infer that the court was unwilling, in a case of such palpable profligacy on the part of the father, to assist him in getting possession of his daughter; and by the terms of the order referring the decision of the question to a barrister, the latter was to determine in whose custody the infant should be permanently placed, and to regulate the access to be had to her by both or either of the parents (*y*).

§ 43. We have noticed the *dictum* of Lord Mansfield, that a Court of Common Law is " not bound to deliver an infant over to any body, nor to give it any privilege;" but it will appear

---

(*y*) At the end of this case (Ib. p. 645) there is added a short note of another, *R.* v. *Wilson*, decided in Hilary Term, 1829. It is, however, too briefly stated to be of much authority. The case is as follows:—" Wife and child, daughter of three years old, brought up by *habeas corpus* sued out by the husband; the wife was asked if she was, under any restraint; and she was told she was at liberty to go where she pleased; and it was referred to the Master to determine at what time and in what manner, and under what circumstances, the father should have access to the daughter; she in the meantime to remain with the mother."

from the following comparatively recent case (z), that this doctrine is not quite correct, and that when a clear right appears, the court does feel itself imperatively called upon to enforce that right, and deliver up the infant to the proper and legal custody. Two persons, named Gregory and Wilkins, had been appointed trustees under the will of Benjamin Harris, the father of two infant children; and he bequeathed to them all his real and personal estate upon trusts for the benefit of those children. The will contained the following clause:—" I appoint the said S. Gregory and W. Wilkins executors of this my last will and testament, and also guardians of the persons and estates of my children; and I earnestly request that my said trustees and executors will, according to their discretion cause my said children to be properly brought up and educated." The children at the time of their father's death were in the custody of J. and G. Isley, their maternal grandfather and grandmother, who refused, when required by the trustees, to give them up; on the ground, that on the death of their mother, five years previously, they had come from America, at the testator's written request, for the purpose of taking care of the children, who were placed under their charge, and had continued with them ever since; and that the father had declared his intention never to remove them so

(z) *R.* v. *Isley*, 5 Ad. & Ell. 441.

long as they were kindly treated. The infants were aged respectively six and nine years, one of them weak in intellect, and both delicate in health and requiring much care.

The guardians obtained a writ of *habeas corpus* (returnable before a Judge at Chambers) commanding J. and G. Isley to bring up the bodies of the infants; and stated in their affidavit that the grandfather and grandmother were very improper persons to have the custody of the children, as they moved in a sphere of life below that to which the expectations of the latter entitled them to aspire: J. Isley had described himself in his affidavit as a " carpenter."

When the parties attended before Patteson, J. at Chambers, the learned Judge, after having taken time for consideration, stated that he felt so much difficulty in the case, that he thought the question ought to be referred to the court in the following term. Shortly afterwards, Isley, the grandfather, and next friend of the children, filed a bill in Chancery on their behalf, against the executors under the will for an account; and also for the purpose of placing the children and their property under the protection of that court. To this the executors put in an answer, before the matter came before the Court of King's Bench.

It was therefore urged that no proceeding for the purpose of changing the custody ought to be entertained, while a bill in Chancery was depending which involved that very question. Lord

Denman, C. J., asked if there was any prospect
of a speedy decision in Chancery; but no answer
was given, except by referring to the affidavit,
which mentioned the fact of the bill having been
filed. The court then made an order that the
defendants should deliver up the bodies of the
children to the guardians.

In delivering judgment Lord Denman, C. J.,
said, "Although we should not consider our discretion tied up if there were a reasonable prospect
of an order of the Court of Chancery being obtained, we think we ought not to make a delay,
which might appear like tampering with the rights
of the guardians. We have, I think, no choice
as to the course we should pursue, but must
order the children to be delivered up to them."

And *per* Littledale, J., "I am of the same
opinion. A guardian appointed as these are is
in the same situation as a parent. We must
enforce the right of the guardians, unless we
could see that the will was made in a manner
contrary to the real wish of the testator. But it
appears that his intention in fact was to remove
the children in the manner which the will points
out. If we saw reason to expect a decision in
Equity on the point, our course of proceeding
might be different." And Patteson, J., added,
" I was not satisfied at Chambers, nor am I yet,
that the father really intended the custody of his
children to be changed. But I think we have no
choice as to our mode of proceeding."

§ 44. It appears then that the Courts of Common Law will put in force the remedial writ of *habeas corpus* on behalf of infants, whenever they are satisfied that they are subject to any illegal or improper restraint; and cruelty or personal ill usage on the part of parents or guardians will be deemed a sufficient ground for their interference. They will also, like the Court of Chancery, protect infants against moral contamination arising from a vicious connection formed by either parent, limiting themselves, however, to cases where that connection is kept up in the presence of the child.   As to general misconduct on the part of the father, it must be very gross before they will interfere (*z*). And although it was laid down by Lord Mansfield that a Court of Common Law is not bound to deliver an infant, when set free from illegal restraint, over *to any body*, in later times it has been held that where a clear right to the custody is shown to exist in any one, the court has no choice, but must order the infant to be delivered up to him.   But even where the application is made by the father, if the order made is simply that the infant shall be discharged from the custody in which it is kept at the time, he will not be allowed to take forcible possession of his child in the presence of the court, or *redeundo* from it.

(*z*) *In re Pulbrook*, 11 Jur. 185.   *In re Fynn*, 12 Jur. 713.

CHAPTER IV.

QUESTION OF CUSTODY WHERE THE INFANT IS ILLEGITIMATE.

§ 45. LET us now see what has been laid down as the law governing the case of *illegitimate* children, bearing in mind the *dictum* of Mr. Justice Patteson, that " the law is perfectly clear as to the right of the father to the possession of his *legitimate* children" (*a*).

On one occasion, Willes, C. J., said (*b*), " He would give no opinion whether the father has any power over a child, who is *nullius filius;* Grotius says truly, that the mother is the only certain parent; and an order of justices to remove the mother always removes the child."

In *R.* v. *Soper* (*c*), Lord Kenyon, C. J., said that the putative father of a bastard child had no right to the custody of it. And when this case was cited in *R.* v. *Moseley* (*d*), where a writ

(*a*) *Ex parte M'Clellan,* 1 Dowl. P. C. 84. *Supra,* p. 11.

(*b*) *Hulland* v. *Malkin,* 2 Wils. 126 ; 1 Bott. P. L. pl. 556 (6th edition).

(*c*) 5 T. R. 278.

(*d*) 5 East, 224 ; and see *R.* v. *Hopkins,* 7 East, 579, and 1 Madd. Ch. Pr. 432, n. (*z*).

of *habeas corpus* was moved for to bring up the body of a bastard infant, of which the defendant was the father, the same learned Judge said, " Where the father has the custody of the child fairly, I do not know that this court would take it away from him; though I do not mean to impeach the propriety of the case cited.   But where he has got possession of the child by force or fraud, as is here suggested, we will interfere to put matters in the same situation as before."

§ 46. In a later case, however, the Court of Common Pleas did take away an infant illegitimate child from the custody in which it had been placed by its father, although there was no imputation against him, and ordered it to be delivered to the mother, who was willing and anxious to receive it (e).   Sir J. Mansfield, C. J., said, " It is not unlikely, indeed, that by granting this application we may be doing a great prejudice to the child, but still *the mother is entitled to the child if she insists upon it* . . . . .   The mother must have the child unless some ground be laid by affidavit to prevent it.   Let the child be delivered to the mother."

It is, however, by no means clear, that such a right on the part of the mother would now be recognised.   In *R.* v. *Hopkins* (f), Lord Ellen-

(e) *Ex parte Knee*, 1 Bos. & Pull. N. R. 148.

(f) 7 East, 579; and see *R.* v. *Felton*, 1 Bott. P. C. pl. 531, where Lord Mansfield said, "neither the putative father nor mother had the legal right of guardianship."

borough expressed a doubt whether the court could interfere by a writ of *habeas corpus* on behalf of the mother of an illegitimate child, who had no legal right to the person of the child, the question of guardianship belonging to another forum, and the child not being of an age to complain for itself of any illegal restraint on its person. As however the infant had been taken away from the mother by force, the court ordered it to be restored to her.

§ 47. The same difficulty was felt and expressed in the following recent case :—An illegitimate child, between eleven and twelve years of age, was produced under the care of a female attendant, by the father with whom it resided, in the Court of Common Pleas, in obedience to a writ of *habeas corpus*, and as he made no claim to the custody, the court allowed the infant to choose for herself the party with whom she wished to remain (g). In delivering judgment, Tindal, C. J. said, " This is a case of some difficulty, and we cannot help feeling distressed at being obliged to come to a decision upon it. The writ of *habeas corpus* has been obtained by the mother of an illegitimate child, for the purpose of bringing her up from the custody of a party with whom she had been placed by her putative father. The child is now in Court in obedience to the writ,

(g) *In re Lloyd,* 3 Man. & Gr. 547.

and appears, as she has been sworn to be, between eleven and twelve years old. *Had she been under seven years of age, the court would have said that she could exercise no discretion ;* but she is old enough to choose for herself, and, therefore, we do not feel called upon to exercise a discretion for her. If she is willing to go with her mother, she may, but if she does so it must be her own free will, for no force shall be used."

His Lordship then asked the child if she would go with her mother, but she expressed a strong disinclination to do so. He then told her that she was at liberty to go where she would; whereupon she left the court with the female who had accompanied her there. Upon quitting the court, the mother attempted to take forcible possession of the child; but upon this being made known to the Chief Justice, one of the officers of the court was sent with her for her protection.

§ 48. Two points in this case are worthy of notice. The child was illegitimate, and the father made no opposition to the mother's claim of custody. With reference to the first, it was asked by Maule, J., "Suppose the infant had been brought up at the instance of a stranger; could the court order her to be given up to him ? *How does the mother of an illegitimate child differ from a stranger?*" And Tindal, C. J., said, " If this had been a young child,"—by which expression the learned Chief Justice seems to have meant within the age of seven years,—" I should feel no difficulty, for the case would then fall within *The King* v. *Hopkins*, where the court returned the child to the custody of the mother. But here the child can speak for herself. Suppose she were to say that she would not go with her mother, we could not force her to do so."

In the course of the argument allusion was made to the new Poor Law Act, 4 & 5 Wm. 4, c. 76, § 71, whereby the burden of supporting a bastard child is thrown upon the mother (*h*); but it was observed by Tindal, C. J., that as the child was born previously to the passing of that statute it did not apply; and Maule, J. called attention to the 57th section of the same statute, which enacts, " that every man who from and after the passing of this act shall marry a woman having a child or children at the time of such marriage, whether such child or children be legitimate or illegitimate, shall be liable to maintain

(*h*) The following is the section referred to:—" And be it further enacted, That every child which shall be born a bastard after the passing of this act shall have and follow the settlement of the mother of such child until such child shall attain the age of sixteen, or shall acquire a settlement in its own right, and such mother, so long as she shall be unmarried or a widow, shall be bound to maintain such child as a part of her family, until such child shall attain the age of sixteen ; and all relief granted to such child while under the age of sixteen shall be considered as granted to such mother : provided always, that such liability of such mother as aforesaid, shall cease on the marriage of such child, if a female."

such child or children as a part of his family, and shall be chargeable with all relief, or the cost price thereof, granted to or on account of such child or children, until such child or children shall respectively attain the age of sixteen, or until the death of the mother of such child or children; and such child or children shall, for the purposes of this act, be deemed a part of such husband's family accordingly." The learned Judge then observed, that according to this clause the applicant's *husband* would appear to be the fit person to have the custody of the child (*i*).

§ 49. The same question also arose lately where a putative father had, previously to the birth of his bastard child, given a bond to the churchwardens and overseers of the parish, conditioned to indemnify them and the inhabitants against all costs and charges arising out of the maintenance of the child (*k*). They brought an action on the bond, and the defendant pleaded that he had been always able and willing to keep and maintain the child; that he had requested

(*i*) In making this enactment, the Legislature seems to have been influenced by the maxim, *Qui sentit commodum sentire debet et onus.*

(*k*) *Bownes* v. *Marsh*, 10 Q. B. 787, and see *Richards* v. *Hodges*, 2 Wms. Saund. 83, where the learned editors say, that within the age of nurture, the putative father certainly has no right to the custody of the child.

G

the churchwardens and overseers to deliver it
over to his care and management, but they had
refused to do so; and that therefore they had
been damnified by their own voluntary act, and
in their own wrong. The plaintiffs, in their
replication, traversed the request of the defendant, and on that issue the verdict was found
for him. Judgment was then moved for *non ob-
stante veredicto*, on the ground that it was not
alleged that the child was willing to go to and be
maintained by the putative father, and that the
latter was not entitled in law to the custody of
his bastard child for the purpose of its care and
management, without its consent thereto, which
consent was not alleged in the plea. On the
part of the defendant it was contended that, as
against the parish officers, the putative father
had a right to the custody of his child, and that
if they persisted in keeping and maintaining the
child contrary to his request, they maintained it
by their own voluntary act, and in their own
wrong. Upon this it was observed by Coleridge,
J., that the argument seemed to assume some
relation between the father and child beyond
what the law acknowledges in the case of illegi-
timacy. The case was, however, decided in
favour of the defendant, on the ground, that as
the plea alleged that the child was under the
power and control of the plaintiffs, and they
refused to deliver her over to the defendant

according to his request, the plaintiffs had no
right to assume, after verdict, that the child was
unwilling to go to the defendant; and, if the
child was indifferent and passive, the facts in the
plea showed that the defendant did not suffer
and permit the child to be maintained by the
parish; he did not suffer and permit that which
was contrary to his express request.

§ 50. The court here did not determine the
point, whether or not the putative father had a
right to insist upon having his child given up to
him for the purpose of maintaining it; but in the
course of the argument it seemed to throw doubt
on the affirmative of that proposition; for Coleridge, J., said, " The question here is, whether,
when a child is beyond the age of nurture, the
parish officers are bound to give it up to the
putative father, from whom they have taken a
bond to maintain it. Suppose the case of a
father whose conduct is notoriously infamous?"
In two former cases, however, of old date, this
right on the part of the father as against the
parish officers was certainly recognised by the
court (*l*); and, at a later period, Chief Justice
Lee and two other Judges declared their opinion,
that the putative father of a bastard child had a
right to maintain it himself, although, in the

(*l*) *Burwell's case*, 1 Ventr. 48; *Sherman's case*, Ib. 210, (temp.
Car. 2).

same case, Foster, J., doubted, and said, that "In his opinion there would be danger of bastard children dying for want of care, or of their being murdered (*m*), if all the putative fathers of such children could take them from the officers of the parishes where they were born, and carry them where they please"(*n*).

There seems to be much force in this observation, and perhaps it will be found, when the point is expressly raised, that the courts will adopt the view, which negatives the *right* of the putative father. It would, however, be hard to make him liable for expenses incurred by the parish, if he is willing to maintain the child himself, and there is no valid ground for impeaching his character or ability. In that case it would seem, that if the parish officers refuse to allow him to have the custody of the child, in order to support it, they can have no claim upon him for reimbursement. But if he is a man of bad character, and one to whom it would be unsafe to entrust the child, then the parish officers might reply that fact to such a plea as was pleaded in *Bownes* v. *Marsh* (*o*), and it would seem to be a sufficient answer, so as, if proved, to entitle them to a verdict.

(*m*) As to cases where want of proper care amounts to murder, see what is said in *Urmston* v. *Newcomen*, 4 Ad. & Ell. 905.

(*n*) *Newland* v. *Osomond*, Sayer, 93 (temp. Geo. 2).

(*o*) *Supra*, p. 81 ; and see *R.* v. *Felton*, 1 Bott. Pl. 531. *Strangeways* v. *Robinson*, 4 Taunt. 498.

§ 51. Where property is left by a putative father to his illegitimate children, and the Master has, under an order of the Court of Chancery, approved of a guardian for them, the court will not allow the mother to remove them, in order that they may reside with her; but will provide that she shall have reasonable access to them, while the care of their education and maintenance is entrusted to the guardian (*p*). The same provident regard for the interests of infants has been shown, by ordering that the representative of the deceased *mother* of an illegitimate child should have free access to it, although the putative father retained the custody and had the care and superintendence of it (*q*). And although a father cannot, under stat. 12 Car. 2, c. 24, appoint a testamentary guardian or guardians for his natural children, yet if he nominates persons in his will to whom he wishes the guardianship of them to be intrusted, the Court of Chancery will in general appoint those persons to the office, provided they are not objectionable on account of their character or circumstances (*r*).

§ 52. By the statute 4 & 5 Phil. & M. c. 3, s. 2, it

(*p*) *Courtois* v. *Vincent*, Jac. 268.

(*q*) *Ord* v. *Blackett*, 9 Mod. 116; see also *Hunter* v. *Macrae*, 5 Hill's MSS. 46; Macpherson on Infants, 112.

(*r*) *Peckham* v. *Peckham*, 2 Cox, 46.   *Ward* v. *St. Paul*, 2 Bro. Ch. Ca. 583. See *Ex parte Glover*, 4 Dowl. 291; Com. Dig. Guardian, (E) 2.

is made unlawful for any person to take or convey
away any maid or woman child, unmarried, being
under the age of sixteen years, " out of or from
the possession, custody, or governance, and
against the will of the father of such maid or
woman child;" and by the third section, if any
person takes or conveys such maid or woman
child, unmarried, out of or from the possession,
and against the will of the father *or mother*, *or of
such person* as shall by lawful means have the
order, keeping, education, or governing of such
child, he is to suffer the punishment of imprison-
ment or fine.   Upon the construction of this
statute it has been held, that it applies to the
case of an illegitimate daughter under the care of
her putative father (*s*).   Indeed, it was said by
one of the Judges who concurred in that decision,
that " The putative father of a natural child has
a natural right to the care and education of
it ; " but from the other authorities that have
been cited it appears that this dictum is incorrect.   The true ground of the judgment was
that, without his consent, the maiden was taken
out of the possession of a person having, by
lawful means, the government and education of
her, which, by the third section, is made an
illegal act.

(*s*) *R.* v. *Cornfort*, 2 Stra. 1162, and S. C. (more fully), in 1
Bott. Pl. 513.

CHAPTER V.

WHERE FORCE OR FRAUD HAS BEEN USED TO GET POSSESSION OF INFANTS.

§ 53. WITH reference to the remedy by writ of *habeas corpus*, and the question, whether there must have been some force or improper restraint previously used, in order to authorize the court to remove an infant from the custody of a party, it is necessary to bear in mind an important distinction. Where the application is made to take away the child from any one *except the father*, it is not a necessary preliminary to show that force or restraint is employed; but there must be some illegal force or improper restraint on the part of the father, in order to enable the court to take away the infant *from him* (a). It was stated by Mr. Justice Patteson in 1831, that there was no instance of the Queen's Bench having taken the custody of the child from the father, on the ground merely of improper instruction (b). And no such case has occurred since that time. The

(a) *Ex parte M'Clellan*, 1 Dowl. 84.
(b) Ib. 85.

proper court to apply to in order to compel a father to perform his duty towards his children, as was said by the same learned Judge, is that of Chancery. It has, however, been previously shown, that in certain cases where the morals of the infant are contaminated, or where it is subjected to personal ill-usage, the Common Law Courts will interfere.

§ 54. But, on the other hand, it is necessary to bear in mind the rule which prevails as to the mode in which a father is justified in getting possession of his infant child. It was laid down by Lord Chancellor King (c), that the father having the undoubted right to the guardianship of his own children, if he can any way gain them, he is at liberty to do so, provided no breach of the peace be made in such an attempt; but the children must not be taken away by him on returning from, any more than coming to, the court, and it will be a contempt in any person offering to do so. And in exact conformity with this principle Lord Eldon said (d), " That a man has a right to the custody of the person of his wife; in general, also, to that of his child; but he must not pursue a legal object by illegal means, as by force of arms, or a conspiracy to do it by force of arms; and though the object is most

(c) *Ex parte Hopkins*, 3 P. Wms. 154.
(d) *De Manneville* v. *De Manneville*, 10 Ves. 62.

legitimate, he may become very criminal by the means used to attain it" (e).

§ 55. We see that in the two last cited *dicta* of learned Judges, the improper means which are specified as vitiating the father's attempt to obtain the custody of his infant child, are *force of arms* and *breach of the peace*, and the same doctrine has been laid down in cases of illegitimate children, where resort has been had to *fraud*. Thus where a putative father, on whom an order of filiation has been made, got possession of the child, three years old, by fraud, Lord Kenyon, C. J., said, " That he had no right to the custody, and the infant was accordingly restored to its mother" (f). This case was followed up by another some years afterwards, in which the same learned Judge upheld the same doctrine, and said (g), "Where the father has the custody of the child fairly, I do not know that this court would take it away from him; though I do not mean to impeach the propriety of the case cited (*R.* v. *Soper*). But where he has got possession of the child by *force or fraud,* as is here suggested, we will interfere to put matters in the same situation as before."

(e) A conspiracy to effect a legal purpose with corrupt intent or by improper means, is an indictable offence. See *R.* v. *Delaval,* 3 Burr. 1435. *R.* v. *Jones,* 4 B. & Ad. 345. *R.* v. *Seward,* 4 Ad. & Ell. 713.   (f) *R.* v. *Soper,* 5 T. R. 278.

(g) *R.* v. *Moseley,* 5 East, 224, n. (a).

§ 56. In illustration of this rule, may be cited the case of *R.* v. *Hopkins* (*h*), where the mother of an infant bastard child applied for a writ of *habeas corpus*, directed to the defendants to bring the child before the court in order that it might be restored to her. It appeared upon affidavits, that the defendants first obtained possession of the infant by stratagem and pretence, but soon afterwards restored it to the mother, from whom it was again taken " by force by Mrs. Hopkins and two soldiers," when it was little more than two years old. Lord Ellenborough, C. J., after some hesitation whether the court could interfere *on behalf of the mother of an illegitimate child, who had no legal right to the custody of its person*, especially as the child, on account of its tender age, was incapable of complaining of any illegal restraint, granted the writ; but on the special ground that improper means had been resorted to for the removal of the infant from its mother. He said, " It appears that the mother of the child, so called, had it in her quiet possession, under her own care and protection, during the period of nurture. That she was first devested of her possession by stratagem, and after recovering it again, was afterwards dispossessed of it by force. In such a case everything is to be presumed in her favour. Without touching, therefore, the question of guardianship, we think

(*h*) 7 East, 579.

that this is a proper occasion for the court, by means of this remedial writ, *to restore the child to the same quiet custody in which it was before the transactions happened* which are the subject of complaint; leaving to the proper forum the decision of any question touching the right of custody and guardianship of this child, with which we do not meddle."

It will be observed how cautiously this decision is worded: it proceeded upon the principle that a Court of Law would not sanction a forcible proceeding to obtain what might *possibly* be the right of a party; but the question of right was left undecided and even untouched, and the writ was granted, as in the case of *R.* v. *Moseley* (*i*), already cited, merely to put matters "in the same situation as before."

§ 57. In the three last cited cases, the infants whose custody was disputed were illegitimate, and as the father in such cases cannot be said to have any legal right to the custody at all, it may be doubted whether the same doctrine as to the use of force or fraud applies to the father of legitimate children. The rule, however, as limited by Lord King and Lord Eldon, namely, that the means employed must be legal and not involve a breach of the peace, is certainly true to this extent, that a father may render himself

(*i*) 5 East, 224, n. (*a*). *Supra*, p. 89.

liable to an indictment by the mode in which he
tries to get possession of his legitimate children.
But even in such a case it by no means follows
that the court will interfere to take his children
away from him when he has once got possession
of them.   This appears from an anonymous
case, cited by Sheppard, Serjt. *arguendo*, in the
case of *Strangeways* v. *Robinson* (*k*), where he
said, that he had once attended as counsel on
behalf of a mother on a writ of *habeas corpus*
before Lord Kenyon, C. J., to prevent a legitimate child, little more than seven years old,
from being carried to the West Indies by his
father; but though the father had obtained the
possession of the child from a school, *both by
fraud and force*, and though Lord Kenyon would
have preferred rather to have left the child in
the custody of the mother, yet he held, that as
he found it in the possession of the father, he
must there leave it.

(*k*) 4 Taunt. 506.

CHAPTER VI.

LIBERTY OF CHOICE ALLOWED TO INFANTS IN QUESTIONS OF CUSTODY.

§ 58. THE next question to consider is, how far any discretion or liberty of choice is permitted to infants with regard to the person to whom their custody is to be committed. And first, as to the practice of the Court of Chancery.

It was once argued at the bar, before Lord Hardwicke, that very little weight should be paid to the inclination of infants, for that it would be very dangerous if they were allowed to have the nomination of their guardian: in such a case a scholar might apply to the court to change his school as not liking it (a). The occasion of this argument was where a father had appointed a female guardian of his daughter, who, being above the age of sixteen, withdrew herself and presented a petition complaining of ill usage and severity on the part of the guardian. The latter was willing to renounce all further interference with the infant, but in conjunction with all the other rela-

(a) *Anon.* 2 Ves. Sen. 374.

tions, wished her to reside with and be under
the care of a Mr. Tracy, who was himself a
relation. The young lady, however, desired that
a Mr. Hexeter, who was merely a neighbour and
no relation, might be the person. The choice
was referred to the Master, who reported in
favour of Mr. Hexeter, chiefly in consequence of
the great disinclination expressed by the infant
against going to Mr. Tracy. On exception to
the report the Lord Chancellor said, that as this
was not a question whether the court should remove a testamentary guardian or not, but only
with whom the infant should reside, and who
should have the personal care of her education,
she being a young lady near seventeen, he thought
that weight should be laid on the inclination of
the infant, and as there was no imputation against
Mr. Hexeter, the exception was disallowed. It
was ordered, however, that the person concerned
in her withdrawing should not have access to
her, and that she should not be married without
leave of the court.

In the course of his judgment, Lord Hardwicke
said, with reference to paying regard to the
wishes of the infant; " In so doing, I ought to
go a little farther than even the law does ; for
supposing there was no testamentary guardian,
nor a mother, if the infant has any socage land,
and is of the age of twelve, if female; of fourteen,
if male; they are allowed to choose their guardians,

as is frequently done on circuit, and is the constant practice, and what this court frequently call on infants to do; though this still is liable to any reasonable objection made to such choice."

§ 59. In the following case it will be seen that this liberty of choice on the part of the infant has been to a certain extent respected even against the father. In the time of Lord Chancellor King, a Mr. Hopkins, who died unmarried and childless, left to each of his three nieces, who resided with him, a considerable sum of money, to be severally paid to them on their respectively attaining the age of twenty-one or marrying, provided that the marriage was with the consent of his three executors (b). One of them was Hopkins, a cousin of the testator, who occupied the house of the latter after his decease and the three nieces continued to live there. Their father (the brother of the testator) presented a petition to the court, setting forth that he had a right to the guardianship of his own children, and praying that they might be delivered over to him. An offer was made to produce an affidavit proving that Hopkins, the cousin, against whom the petition was exhibited, "had been often seen to kiss the eldest niece, and to go into her chamber; and that there was reason to suspect him of some intentions to inveigle her affections in order to a marriage."

(b) *Ex parte Hopkins*, 2 P. Wms. 152. *Supra*, p. 38. 88.

At this period the eldest girl was only thirteen years of age. The Lord Chancellor asked the eldest daughter, who was in court, whether she was under any force, and where she would rather be? She replied, that she was not under any force; and that, though she had all imaginable duty for her father and mother, yet her uncle, the testator, having been so kind to her by his will, she thought herself under an obligation to continue where he intended she should, and that she thought it to be his intention she should continue in the house where he himself had placed her. Whereupon the Lord Chancellor dismissed the petition; but directed Mr. Hopkins, who had the young ladies in his custody, to permit their father and mother, at all seasonable times, to have access to and see their children (c).

§ 60. The rule that prevails in Courts of Common Law upon this subject was laid down with precision in a case of no distant date, which has been already cited (d). There Lord Denman,

(c) In a note upon this case, it is stated by Cox, the editor of the 5th edition, that if the parties brought up upon a writ of *homine replegiando* or *habeas corpus*, will acquaint the court, that they are under no force, the court will let them go back to the places from whence they came; or if they appear to be under restraint will set them at liberty, but not deliver them into the custody of another, nor in a proceeding of that nature determine private rights, as the right of guardianship evidently is. See, however, *Eyre* v. *Countess of Shaftesbury*, 2 P. Wms. 103, and *R.* v. *Isley*, 5 Ad. & Ell. 441. *Supra*, p. 72.

(d) *R.* v. *Greenhill*, 4 Ad. & Ell. 624. *Supra*, p. 66.

C. J., explicitly stated the law, "because any
doubts left on the minds of the public as to the
right to claim the custody of children might lead
to dreadful disputes, and even endanger the lives
of persons at the most helpless age." He said,
" When an infant is brought before the court by
habeas corpus, if he be of an age to exercise a
choice, the court leaves him to elect where he
will go. If he be not of that age, and a want of
direction would only expose him to dangers or
seductions, the court must make an order for his
being placed in the proper custody (*e*). The only
question then is, what is to be considered the
proper custody ; and that undoubtedly is the
custody of the father. The court has, it is true,
intimated that the right of the father would not
be acted upon where the enforcement of it would
be attended with danger to the child; as where
there was an apprehension of cruelty, or of contamination by some gross profligacy." And the
following account of the course to be adopted
was on the same occasion given by Mr. Justice
Littledale. " The practice in such cases is that,
if the children be of a proper age, the court gives
them their election as to the custody in which
they will be ; if not, the court takes care that
they be delivered into the proper custody. If
this were a case in which the father and mother
disagreed as to the disposal of the children, and

(*e*) See *supra*, section 43, and *infra*, sections 64, 65.

H

they were brought from a distant place in the charge of some other person, and each of the parents appeared before the court, and claimed the custody, there is no doubt that the court would give it to the father; the mother's application would not be attended to. Here the case is stronger; the children were, in effect, in the custody of the father, in a place selected by him; they have been removed and he only seeks to bring them back."

§ 61. Another instance in which the court respected the wishes of an infant, who was competent to exercise a sound discretion, occurred in the case of *R.* v. *Clarkson* (*e*), where a man pretending that he was married to a young lady of fortune, obtained a writ of *habeas corpus*, directed to her guardians commanding them to produce her in court. On the return to this writ, it appeared that she had, under her mother's will, been committed to the care of the defendant, who had placed her at a school where she was quite willing to remain of her own accord. When she was brought into court, the Chief Justice (Sir John Pratt), asked her if she desired to be taken out of the hands of the persons she lived with and go with the party who claimed her as his wife. She denied that he was her husband, and desired that she might continue with her guardian. Upon this, it was said *per curiam,*

(*e*) 1 Strange, 444.

that they had nothing to do to order her to go with Dibley, the pretended husband, but only to see that she was under no illegal restraint; " all we can do is, to declare that she is at liberty to go where she pleases; but lest this writ be made use of by Dibley, as a means to get her abroad, and seize her, we will order our tipstaff to wait upon her home to her guardians; and so it was done in *Lady Harriet Berkeley's case.*"

§ 62. Of the case of Lady Harriet Berkeley here referred to, Lord Mansfield subsequently said (*f*) that *R.* v. *Clarkson* bears no resemblance to it, " as the reporter has made the court declare." It occurred in the reign of Charles 2nd, and was an indictment against Lord Grey and others for a conspiracy in carrying away that lady, " then a virgin, unmarried, within the age of eighteen years," out of the custody of her father the Earl of Berkeley, and causing her to cohabit with Lord Grey, he being at the time the husband of one of her sisters. The trial was one at bar, and when the jury withdrew to consider their verdict the following scene took place (*g*).

" *Earl of Berkeley.*—My Lord Chief Justice, I desire I may have my daughter delivered to me again.

Lord Chief Justice.—My Lord Berkeley must have his daughter again.

(*f*) *R.* v. *Delaval,* 1 W. Bl. 412.   (*g*) State Trials, 9. 183.

H 2

Lady Henrietta.—I will not go to my father again.

Justice Holben.—My Lord, she being now in court, and there being a *homine replegiando* against my Lord Grey, for her, upon which he was committed, we must now examine her. Are you under any custody or restraint, Madam?

Lady Henrietta.—No, my Lord, I am not.

Lord Chief Justice.—Then we cannot deny my Lord Berkeley the custody of his own daughter.

Lady Henrietta.—My Lord, I am married.

Lord Chief Justice.—To whom?

Lady Henrietta.—To Mr. Turner.

Lord Chief Justice.—What Turner? Where is he?

Lady Henrietta.—He is here in court.

Lord Chief Justice.—My Lord Berkeley, your daughter is free for you to take her; as for Mr. Turner, if he thinks he has any right to the lady, let him take his course. Are you at liberty and under no restraint?

Lady Henrietta.—I will go with my husband.

Earl of Berkeley.—Hussey, you shall go with me home.

Lady Henrietta.—I will go with my husband.

Earl of Berkeley.—Hussey, you shall go with me, I say.

Lady Henrietta.—I will go with my husband.

Earl of Berkeley.—My Lord, I desire I may have my daughter again.

Lord Chief Justice.—My Lord, we do not hinder you, you may take her.

Lady Henrietta.—I will go with my husband.

Earl of Berkeley.—Then all that are my friends seize her I charge you.

Lord Chief Justice.—Nay, let us have no breaking of the peace in the court.

Then the court broke up, and passing through the hall there was a great scuffle about the lady, and swords drawn on both sides, but my Lord Chief Justice coming by, ordered the tipstaff that attended him (who had formerly a warrant to search for her and take her into custody) to take charge of her, and carry her over to the King's Bench; and Mr. Turner asking if he should be committed too, the Chief Justice told him, he might go with her if he would, which he did, and as it is reported, they lay together that night in the Marshal's house, and she was released out of prison, by order of the court, the last day of the term" (*h*).

§ 63. The infant, however, must be capable of exercising a sound discretion upon the question, and this of course will depend upon its age and its degree of intelligence which varies in so remarkable a manner in different children.   In a very

(*h*) On the question of protection afforded by the court to prevent a seizure either in court or *redeundo*, see *R.* v. *Mead*, 1 Burr. 542. *R.* v. *Brook*, 4 Burr. 1991. *Re Douglas*, 3 Q. B. 831.

recent case (*i*), where Mr. Justice Patteson refused
an application for a writ of *habeas corpus*, made
on behalf of an infant's mother, then in India, (the
father being dead), in order to remove her son from
the guardianship of persons who had for some time
had the custody of him, the learned Judge said,
" In deciding this question it seems to me it is
altogether useless to question the child, as to
with whom he might wish to be. *It is difficult to
say at what age a child is capable of exercising a
sound discretion, and judging for itself in matters
of this kind (j)*; but it seems to me that it is but
a mockery to ask a child of nine years of age,
whether he would sooner remain with the person who has brought him up, or go with a
stranger" (*k*).

§ 64. The view here taken by the learned
Judge as to the inability of an infant of the age
of nine years to exercise a proper discretion on
such a question, is in accordance with what
was laid down by the Court of King's Bench in

(*i*) *In re Preston*, 5 Dowl. & L. 247.

(*j*) Between the ages of seven and fourteen years an infant is
deemed *primâ facie* to be *doli incapax*; but this presumption may
be rebutted by strong proof of a mischievous discretion, for then
the maxim applies that *malitia supplet ætatem.* 1 Hale, P. C. 25. 27.
It is mentioned in a note to Hale's P. C. 1. 25, that at Abingdon
Assizes, Feb. 23rd, 1629, an infant between eight and nine years
was convicted of arson and hanged.

. (*k*) And see per Tindal, C. J., in *Re Ann Lloyd*, 3 Man. & Gr.
548.

the reign of George I., in a case where a female child nine years old was brought up by *habeas corpus* in the custody of its nurse (*l*). And it was moved that she might be discharged if she was under any restraint, which was agreed to, but it appeared she was not. The father's will was then produced, whereby he had devised the custody of her to her uncle, and an application was made that she might be delivered up to him as her guardian. The court at first doubted whether they should go any farther than to see that the child was under no illegal restraint; but afterwards declared that *this being the case of a young child who had no judgment of her own*, they ought to deliver her to her guardian, who took possession of her in court.

It will be observed, however, that here the proposition as to the incapacity of an infant of nine years of age to judge for itself is asserted more absolutely than in *Re Preston*, for there Mr. Justice Patteson seems to have laid stress upon the fact that a child of such tender years would, without doubt, if asked the question, prefer the society to which it was accustomed to that of a stranger, and that, therefore, it would be idle to propose it; but the court, in *R.* v. *Johnson*, said, without any reference to the predilections of habit, that a child of that age had no judgment of its own.

But although similar reasons are assigned for

(*l*) *R.* v. *Johnson*, 1 Stra. 579. S. C. 2 Ld. Raym. 1333.

these two decisions the results were different; for in the former case, the infant was allowed to *remain* in the custody of the persons who had previously taken charge of it; in the latter, the infant was *removed* from the custody of its nurse to that of its guardian.

§ 65. It is right, however, to notice that in a later case (*m*), which came before Lord Hardwicke, C. J., and the rest of the Court of King's Bench, it was said by Lee, J., that Lord Raymond, who had been a party to the judgment of the court in *R.* v. *Johnson*, repented of what was done in that case. But Lord Mansfield, at a subsequent period, declared his opinion, and that of the court, that the decision in *R.* v. *Johnson* was correct. He observed (*n*), "It is said in the next case (*R.* v. *Smith*) that Lord Raymond repented of what was done in this (*R.* v. *Johnson*). His Lordship was latterly a very scrupulous man. But we are clear his first judgment was the right one." In *R.* v. *Smith* (*m*), a boy between thirteen and fourteen years old, who was living with his aunt, was brought up by *habeas corpus at the suit of his father*. The reporter says, "And now upon debate that case

<hr/>

(*m*) *R.* v. *Smith*, Stra. 982.

(*n*) *R.* v. *Delaval*, 1 W. Bl. 412. 3 Burr. 1434, S. C. It is necessary to compare carefully these two reports, as they do not quite correspond.

(*R* v. *Johnson*) was overruled." The court decided that upon the writ of *habeas corpus* they could only deliver the child out of the custody of the aunt, and inform him he was at liberty to go where he pleased, and they said, that was all that was done in *Lady Catharine Annesley's case;* that the right of guardianship could not be determined by them in this summary way, and the father was not without other remedy; he might have trespass *quare filium et hæredem suum rapuit,* or other actions that would properly bring the right of guardianship in question.

§ 66. It will be observed, that it is incorrect to say, that by this judgment the case of *R.* v. *Johnson* was overruled, for there the decision which delivered the child over to her guardian, proceeded expressly upon the ground that she was so young (her age being nine years), that she had no judgment of her own; whereas, in *R.* v. *Smith,* the boy was within six weeks of fourteen, and, consequently, capable of exercising a discretion, which the court respected, and gave effect to. And Lord Mansfield, in the same judgment in which he upheld the ruling in *R.* v. *Johnson,* reviewed the three cases of *R.* v. *Clarkson* (*o*), *R.* v. *Johnson,* and *R.* v. *Smith,* and said, " We have considered those cases very fully. We think what was done in all of them was very

(*o*) Stra. 444. *Supra*, p. 98.

right; but we don't agree with what was said in the books about them." With regard to *R.* v. *Smith*, his Lordship said, "That case was determined right (barring the dictums that were used in it) for the court was certainly right in refusing to deliver the infant to the father, of whose design in applying for the custody of his child they had a bad opinion." And he added, "The true rule is, that the court are to judge of the circumstances of the particular case, and to give their directions accordingly" (*p*).

Very recently an illegitimate child, seven years old, about whose custody there was a dispute in the Bail Court, was called up to the Bench by Mr. Justice Wightman, and after having been privately questioned by him and found to be very intelligent, she was allowed to choose the person, although neither her father nor mother, with whom she was to reside. It was, however, agreed, that the mother should have access to her at all reasonable times (*q*).

(*p*) 3 Burr. 1437. In the report in 1 W. Bl. 413, the rule is given thus, " Upon the whole, the true rule to be collected from all these cases is, that if the circumstances require a change of the custody, it must be delivered in court. If they do not require it, the privilege *redeundo* is of course." It must be admitted that the statement in Burrow is the most clear and intelligible of the two.

(*q*) *In re White*, Jan. 25, 1848, not reported.

CHAPTER VII.

LAW OF CUSTODY IN CASES OF GUARDIANSHIP.

§ 67. As the object of this work is not to treat
of the rights which belong to, nor of the duties
which devolve upon those who are appointed
guardians of infants in any other respect than
as bearing upon the question of custody of the
person, resort must be had by those who wish to
make themselves fully acquainted with the law
of guardianship to other treatises, which have
entered at large upon the subject (*a*).

Nor is it necessary here to discuss the different
kinds of guardianship, whether in Chivalry, in
Socage, by Custom, by Nature, or for Nurture (*b*),
respecting which much of the old law has either
become obsolete, or has seldom any practical
application at the present day. The last two
kinds here mentioned may, in one sense, be said
to embrace generally the question of parental

(*a*) See, especially, the first part of Macpherson's Law relating
to Infants, where the whole question is discussed with much
learning and accuracy. See also Chambers on the Jurisdiction of
the Court of Chancery over Infants.

(*b*) See the very learned notes of Hargrave, Co. Litt. 88, *b*.

rights; but they have a technical meaning different from this. Guardianship by Nature properly applies only to the case of the custody of the heir apparent, who is entitled to lands by descent and this is quite distinct from the natural guardianship of all his children, to which a father is entitled during their minority (c).

Guardianship for or by Nurture only occurs where the infant is without any other guardian, and none can have it except the father or mother. It extends no further than the custody and government of the infant's person, and determines at the age of fourteen in the case both of males and females (d).

§ 68. Where the father is dead, and no other guardian has been legally appointed, the mother is guardian for nurture of each of her children, until they attain that age. If a guardian for nurture delivers over the infant to another for instruction, he may afterwards retake him into his own custody, although it has been said, that if he grants the infant (i. e. the custody) to another, that binds himself, so that he cannot claim the custody as against the grantee (e).

The father is, no doubt, while he lives, the natural guardian of his children during their

(c) See Macpherson on Infants, Part 1, 64.
(d) Bro. *Garde*, 70. *Ratcliff's case*, 3 Rep. 37, n. (13); Co. Litt. 88, b.
(e) Com. Dig. Guardian (D).

minority (f), nor can another be appointed guardian during his life, " although, in certain cases, a person may be nominated *to act as* guardian" (g). On the death of the father, without any appointment by him of a testamentary guardian, the mother has been declared to be guardian of the minor children by nature (h). She has, in such a case, a right to the custody of the person and care of the education of her children; it is a natural right, " and this in all countries," said Lord Hardwicke, "where the laws do not break in" (i).

§ 69.   But the right of the mother is absolutely defeated, where the father, under the powers given to him by stat. 12 Car. 2, c. 24, appoints by deed or will another person to be the guardian of his children.   For by section 8 of that statute it is enacted, " that where any person hath or shall or have any child or childen under the age of one and twenty years, and not married at the time of his death, that it shall and may be lawful to and for the father of such child or children, whether born at the time of the decease of the father, or that time in *ventre sa*

(f) *Stileman* v. *Ashdown*, 2 Atk. 480.   Lord Hardwicke there says " sons," but see per Lord Eldon, in *De Manneville* v. *De Manneville*, 10 Ves. 62.

(g) Per Lord Eldon, *Ex parte Mountfort*, 15 Ves. 447.

(h) *Eyre* v. *Countess of Shaftesbury*, 2 P. Wms. 116.   *Infra*, § 71.

(i) *Villareal* v. *Mellish*, 2 Swanst. 536.

mère, or whether such father be within the age of one and twenty years, or of full age, by deed executed in his lifetime, or by his last will and testament in writing, in the presence of two or more credible witnesses, in such manner, and from time to time as he shall respectively think fit, to dispose of the custody and tuition of such child or children, for and during such time as he or they shall respectively remain under the age of one and twenty years, or any lesser time, to any person or persons in possession or remainder, other than popish recusants; and that such dis- position of the custody of such child or children, made since the 24th of February, 1645, or here- after to be made, shall be good and effectual against all and every person or persons claiming the custody or tuition of such child or children as guardian in socage or otherwise; and that such person or persons, to whom the custody of such child or children hath been or shall be so dis- posed or devised as aforesaid, shall and may maintain an action of ravishment of ward, or tres- pass, against any person or persons which shall wrongfully take away or detain such child or children, for the recovery of such child or children; and shall and may recover damages for the same in the said action, for the use and benefit of such child or children."

§ 70. Under this act the father alone has the

power of appointing a guardian; and where the will under which he nominated a party to that office was not duly executed, the Court of Exchequer on one occasion (sitting as a Court of Equity) so far respected his wishes as to appoint that party the guardian without any reference to the Master (*k*). The mother, however, has no such power, and an appointment by her is void (*l*). Neither can the guardian delegate the trust to another; it is a matter of personal confidence, and, therefore, not assignable, and will not pass to his executors or administrators (*m*). " Such testamentary guardian takes place of all other guardians, and his interest is for the good and honour of the family; as the father was the head of the family, so the statute puts him *in loco patris*" (*n*). He, therefore, has the power of determining at what school or university the minor shall be educated; and where an infant went to Oxford contrary to the orders of his guardian, who preferred Cambridge, a messenger was sent by the court to take him to the latter place. The young man, however, got back to Oxford, upon which, as the report quaintly ex-

(*k*) *Hall* v. *Storer*, 1 Y. & Coll. 556. See also in the case of an illegitimate child, *supra*, p. 85.

(*l*) *Bedell* v. *Constable*, Vaughan, 180. *Ex parte Edwards*, 3 Atk. 519.

(*m*) Ib. 179. *Lady Teynham's case*, 4 Bro. Parl. Ca. 302. *Eyre* v. *Countess of Shaftesbury*, 2 P. Wms. 121.

(*n*) Ib. 124. See also per Littledale, J., in *R.* v. *Isley*, 5 Ad. & Ell. 448.

presses it, " there went another (messenger) *tam*
to carry him to Cambridge *quam* to keep him
there " (*o*).

§ 71. Where several guardians are appointed
by the father under the powers given by stat. 12
Car. 2, c. 24, s. 8, even although there are no
words of survivorship in the instrument of appointment, yet the office belongs to the survivor.
Upon this question the case of Mr. Justice Eyre
against the Countess of Shaftesbury (*p*) presents
some interesting features.   The Earl of Shaftesbury devised by will the guardianship of the person
and estate of his infant son to Mr. Justice Eyre
and two other persons (both of whom were dead
before the commencement of the suit), without
adding the words, " *and to the survivor of them.*"
When the young earl was twelve years of age,
the plaintiff, perceiving that his mother had not
provided a proper tutor for him, petitioned the
Lord Chancellor (Lord Macclesfield), that the
person of the infant might be delivered over
to him as sole surviving guardian.   In opposition to the claim it was, amongst other objections, argued, that in this case the guardianship did not survive, for want of express words
in the will to that effect.   The Lord Chancellor,
however, said, that where three guardians are

(*o*) *Tremaine's case*, Stra. 168, and see *Hall* v. *Hall*, 3 Atk. 721.
(*p*) 2 P. Wms. 104; and see *Wright* v. *Naylor*, 5 Madd. 77.

appointed by will, each of them seems to be a complete guardian, like the case where there are two or three churchwardens of a parish, each of them is a distinct churchwarden ; and that it would be mischievous and of very ill effect, if, where there are several guardians appointed by will, and some refuse to act, the rest should not be able to do anything; and yet this must be the consequence, if a guardianship devised to several should be taken to be one joint naked authority. He added, that the father has, by the statute, 12 Car. 2, c. 24, a right to dispose of the guardianship of his child until twenty-one, and having done so here, it would be binding, unless some misbehaviour were shown in the guardian, in which case, it being a matter of trust, the Court of Chancery had a superintendency over it. He, therefore, made an order that the infant should be delivered into the hands of the guardian, "who desired the young earl might dine with him. But the Lord Chancellor said, that was in confidence that the Judge should return him to his mother, the countess, at night, for that, as yet, the court could not make any order touching the custody of the earl's person" (*q*).

Afterwards, when the Great Seal was taken from Lord Macclesfield on the occasion of his

(*q*) Lord Macclesfield added, " But I must differ from Mr. Justice Eyre, as to sending the infant to a public school, *which may be thought likely to instil into him notions of slavery*."

I

disgrace, the same plaintiff, then Lord Chief
Baron Eyre, exhibited a petition to the Lords
Commissioners, in which he stated, that the infant earl, then just fourteen years of age, had
been married, without the consent or privity of
the Lord Chief Baron, his surviving guardian,
and was detained from him. He prayed, therefore, that the custody or tuition of the infant
might be granted to him.

The earl also presented a petition, praying
that he might be at liberty himself to choose his
own guardian.

The court made an order that the person of
the infant should be restored by the countess, his
mother, to the Lord Chief Baron; and they said,
that although the declaration made by the late
Lord Chancellor, that the right of guardianship
did belong to the petitioner as surviving guardian,
and the order made thereupon, were ever so erroneous, yet that the same was a good order until
reversed, and, consequently, it was a contempt to
break it.

§ 72. With reference to the claims of the
mother in such a case, it may be laid down that
the right of a testamentary guardian is paramount
as against her, and she has no right to interfere
with his discretion in respect of the custody and
education of the minor children. It had been
argued in the above case on behalf of the

countess, that there was no instance on record where a complaint had been made in court against an infant's mother, for taking away her own child. But it was answered by the Lords Commissioners, that the guardians of the infant Duke of Hamilton petitioned against the Duchess of Hamilton for taking away the infant duke out of their custody, and their complaint was received; upon which the court would have proceeded against the mother, but the guardians could not make out their right of guardianship, by reason of some defect in the instrument under which they claimed. And as in the principal case the Lords Commissioners held, that the Countess Dowager of Shaftesbury had been guilty of a contempt in contriving and effecting the marriage of the infant son without the consent of the guardian, and without applying to the court, they ordered that a sequestration should issue against her.

On a late occasion (r), the law with regard to the conflicting claims of a testamentary guardian and a mother, was explicitly laid down by Lord Chancellor Cottenham, who said, " It is proper that mothers of children thus circumstanced should know that they have no right, as such, to interfere with testamentary guardians, and if under the peculiar circumstances, I think it

(r) *Talbot* v. *Earl of Shrewsbury*, 4 Myl. & Cr. 683.

proper now to leave the child in the custody of
the mother, it is not in respect of right in that
mother, but it is in consequence of that power
which the court has of controlling the power of
testamentary guardians."

§ 73. In the case of female infants this testamentary guardianship determines on their marriage, but continues in the case of males until
the age of twenty-one notwithstanding that
event (s).

§ 74. Over all guardians, whether testamentary or appointed by the Court of Chancery, that
court will exercise efficient control, and interpose its authority whenever there is reasonable
ground for apprehension that the interests of
infants are likely to suffer injury, or a particular
place or course of education is deemed proper for
them.   Lord Chancellor Macclesfield on one occasion (t), " with some warmth" said, that the guardians were but trustees, and that the court would
and had interposed even in the case of a father;

(s) *Mendes* v. *Mendes*, 1 Ves. 91 ; and see *Roach* v. *Garvan*, Ib.
160. *Eyre* v. *Countess of Shaftesbury*, 2 P. Wms. 109.
(t) *Duke of Beaufort* v. *Berty*, 1 P. Wms. 704, 705 ; and see
Roach v. *Garvan*, 1 Ves. 160. *Storke* v. *Storke*, 3 P. Wms. 51.
Talbot v. *Earl of Shrewsbury*, 4 Myl. & Cr. 683. Lord Nottingham, however, in *Foster* v. *Denny*, 2 Bro. Ch. Ca. 237, with reference to a testamentary guardian said, that he could not *remove* a
guardian by act of Parliament. See also *Ingham* v. *Bickerdike*, 6
Madd. 275. *Dillon* v. *Lady Mount Cashel*, 4 Bro. Par. Ca. 306.

that preventing justice was to be preferred to punishing justice; and that he ought rather to prevent the mischief and misbehaviour of guardians, than to punish it when done. That if any wrong steps had been taken which might not deserve punishment, yet if they were such as induced the least suspicion of the infants being like to suffer by the conduct of the guardians, or if the guardians chose to make use of methods that might turn to the prejudice of the infant, the court would interpose, and order the contrary; and that this was grounded upon the general power and jurisdiction which it had over all trusts, and a guardianship was most plainly a trust.

§ 75. This controlling power of the court over testamentary guardians was exercised in the following case (*u*):—H. G. by will made H. C. and T., guardians of his infant daughter, desiring them to take care of her and her estate during her minority. C. educated the daughter under him while he lived; but after his death, she was placed at a boarding school by the surviving guardians; when H. took her from the school (she being then of the age of nine years and three months) and married her to his own son F. H., who had no estate, and was apprentice to a peruke maker. A motion was made in the

(*u*) *Goodall* v. *Harris*, 2 P. Wms. 561.

Court of Chancery on the subject, and the parties were ordered to attend, when Lord Chancellor King said, " The infant girl never having been under the care of the court, nor committed by the court to the custody of the defendant H., I do not think this an immediate contempt of the court; but then it is a very ill thing in the guardian to marry this child to his own son, and punishable by an information; and I will have this guardian bound over with sureties to be taken by the Master, to appear and answer to an information to be exhibited by the Attorney General against him.

    As to the child, let her be delivered over by this knavish guardian to the other guardian T., but he being at present in the country, the child shall be placed with the plaintiff's clerk in court, to be by him delivered to T., who (it is to be presumed) will act, as he has not yet renounced the guardianship; and let it be done this afternoon, otherwise H., the guardian, to stand committed."

    Where a testamentary guardian declines to act, a guardian may be appointed on petition (v); but a testamentary guardian cannot be *removed* for misconduct without bill (w).

(v) *O'Keefe* v. *Casey*, 1 Scho. & Lef. 106. See *In re Johnstone*, 2 Jon. & Lat. 222.

(w) *O'Keefe* v. *Casey*, 1 Scho. & Lef. 106. *In re McCullochs*, 1 Dru. 276. As to what is a sufficient appointment of a testa-

§ 76. A case of some importance bearing upon the subject of the rights of a joint testamentary guardian was recently decided (*x*).   An action of trespass was brought by the mother of two infants against the servants of a party, who was with her a joint testamentary guardian of them, for taking them out of her custody; and the declaration stated, that the defendants assaulted one F. S. G. and one J. G., then being the sons and servants of the plaintiff, and forcibly took them away from her, *per quod servitia amisit.* The defendants pleaded that the said F. S. G. and J. G. (the infants in question) were the lawful issue of the plaintiff and one J. M. G., and that the latter by a codicil to his will, directed that W. G. should be a guardian of the said F. S. G. and J. G., "with a certain person therein in that behalf named." The plea then after alleging the death of J. M. G. and the acceptance of the trust by W. G. whereby he became lawful guardian with the said other person of the children, stated, that the children were under the age of eight years and above the age of four, and were in the custody of the plaintiff as such servants, as in the declaration mentioned, and that she had them in her custody without the license

mentary guardian, see *Ex parte Earl of Ilchester*, 7 Ves. 348. *Miller* v. *Harris*, 14 Sim. 540.

(*x*) *Gilbert* v. *Schwenck*, 14 M. & W. 488. See also *Campbell* v. *Mackay*, 2 Myl. & Cr. 37.

or consent and against the will of the said W. G., who was desirous of having the care and custody of them. The plea then justified the act complained of, as done by them as servants of the said W. G., and by his command, that he might have the care and custody of the children. To this there was a replication, that the said W. G. was appointed joint guardian with the plaintiff, she being the said " other person" named in the codicil. The defendant specially demurred to this replication, but the chief point insisted upon in argument was, that no action would lie by the testamentary guardian against the defendants for taking out of her custody a child, in whom the party by whose authority they acted, had, as co-guardian with her, a joint interest. On the other side it was contended, that the plea was bad in substance, for it admitted that the children were the servants of the plaintiff; and if so, the testamentary guardian could not take infants out of the custody of their *master* or *mistress*, and so destroy the contract of service. In delivering the judgment of the court, Parke, B. said, " The solution of this question depends upon the nature of the power which, at the time of the alleged trespass, vested in W. G., by virtue of his appointment of joint guardian.

Guardians appointed by will, according to the statute of 12 Car. 2, c. 24, have no more power than guardians in socage, and are but trustees.

This doctrine is recognised in *The Duke of Beaufort* v. *Berty* (*y*), and *Frederick* v. *Frederick* (*z*). But one of two joint trustees cannot act in the trust in defiance of the will of the other; each has an equal power. It seems to follow, that as the children were in the custody of the plaintiff, and in a service which, upon these pleadings, must be taken to have been in its nature lawful, the defendants, as the servants of W. G., were not justified in removing them against the plaintiff's will.

It is unnecessary to discuss the effect of the plaintiffs being, in the absence of any appointment of testamentary guardian, the natural guardian of the infants."

§ 77. Where testamentary guardians are appointed, the court will, notwithstanding, take into account the wishes of the deceased father as to the place and mode of education of his children. Lord Cottenham said, " that the law will pay the highest respect to the expression of his wishes" on this point (*a*). But at the same time care will be taken not to disregard the rights of the testamentary guardian, even while carrying into effect the wishes of the testator, and in adjusting this matter nice and delicate questions may fre-

---

(*y*) 1 P. Wms. 703.   (*z*) Ib. 721.
(*a*) *Campbell* v. *Mackay*, 2 Myl. & Cr. 34; see also *Talbot* v. *Earl of Shrewsbury*, 4 Myl. & Cr. 683, 684.

quently arise. Thus a father appointed two persons guardians of his infant children, and "recommended" that if his wife should die before his son should attain the age of twenty-one, or before his daughters should attain that age or marry, the guardians should place such of them as should then be minors under the care of his cousin M. P., to be assisted by their aunt S. B. (*b*). After the death of the mother, a suit was instituted by the maternal grandfather in the names of the infants for the purpose of making them wards of court; and a petition was presented by him, and an order made by the Vice Chancellor of England, referring it to the Master to settle a scheme for their education and management. This scheme provided that they should forthwith be placed under the care and be maintained and educated under the direction of M. P. assisted by S. B.

To this the surviving testamentary guardian objected, partly on account of the distance of the proposed place of residence from his own home, and partly because the two ladies were dissenters from the church of England. The Lord Chancellor (Lord Cottenham), however, said, that although he was clearly of opinion that they had no claim whatever to the character of testamentary guardians, yet it was certain that the testator had expressed a wish with respect to

(*b*) *Knott* v. *Cottee*, 2 Phill. 192.

them, which the court, no less than the testamentary guardian was bound to attend to. But, he asked, "is the testamentary guardian to have no supervision as to the mode in which the money allowed for the maintenance and education of the children is to be expended? I cannot think that that is consistent with the testator's intention." The Lord Chancellor then said, "What occurs to me on this point is this; I see no objection to leaving the immediate custody of the children to Miss P., who, being with the children, may be better able to judge what they actually want; but that there should be no change of residence and no change of governess without communication with the testamentary guardian. I think it will be better not to give him the control, but to give him information, in order that he may, if he thinks there is a case for it, come to the court for direction; and also that half-yearly accounts should be rendered to him, as to the mode in which the allowance has been expended for the benefit of the children; for I think that is a right which he has as testamentary guardian. This, I think, will give him as much control and superintendence as the testator intended he should have, while it will give effect to the expressed wish of the testator as to the persons to whom the immediate care of the children should be intrusted" (c).

(c) See *Talbot* v. *Earl of Shrewsbury*, 4 Myl. & Cr. 684.

§ 78. In the *case of the Earl of Ilchester*, Lord Eldon laid down some wise rules to be observed by the guardian, in respecting the wishes of the mother in the execution of his important and responsible office. He said (*d*), "In this case I need not add, that though the effect of the appointment of a guardian is to commit the custody of the guardianship, this court looks with great anxiety to the execution of the duty belonging to the guardian, and the attention expected to be paid to the reasonable wishes of the natural parent. Though it is not necessary in this instance, upon such a contest it is important to observe, that it can never end happily but by implanting in the hearts of the children filial and dutiful feelings towards the parent; the best and most important duty imposed upon the guardian by the deceased parent."

§ 79. The next subject to consider is the case of guardians appointed by the Court of Chancery.

We have already noticed the rule laid down by Lord Eldon, that to enable that court to interfere in the care of infants, they must have property, not from any want of jurisdiction on the part of the court, but from the want of means to exercise its jurisdiction with effect (*e*). This,

(*d*) 7 Ves. 381.

(*e*) *Supra*, p. 16. See also the observations of Vice Chancellor Knight Bruce, in *Re Fynn*, 12 Jur. 720.

however, must not be understood as meant to apply to cases where the court is merely called upon in the exercise of its common law right to issue a writ of *habeas corpus*, to relieve against an improper custody; but only where something further is required, such as provision to be made with respect to the education and maintenance of the infant. Otherwise there would be no force in the reason assigned by Lord Eldon for the limitation which he draws, for the absence of property in the infant cannot constitute " a want of means to exercise the jurisdiction" of the court, where all that is required is removal from illegal or improper restraint of the person. And it should have been in a previous part of the work mentioned, that the same distinction seems to be observed in favour of infants, where the application is simply by petition that they may be delivered up to the proper custody. In a recent case of the latter kind (*f*), where it was contended that the Court of Chancery had no jurisdiction over infants, distinct from that at common law upon *habeas corpus*, unless there was some property to be administered for the infants' benefit, Lord Chancellor Cottenham said, " I have no doubt about the jurisdiction. The cases in which the court interferes on behalf of infants, are not confined to those in which there is property. Courts of law interfere by *habeas*

(*f*) *In re Spence*, 2 Phillips, 247.

for the protection of the person of *any* body who is suggested to be improperly detained (*g*). This court interferes for the protection of infants, *qua* infants, by virtue of the prerogative which belongs to the crown as *parens patriæ*, and the exercise of which is delegated to the Great Seal." By attention to the distinction which has been above pointed out, we may without difficulty reconcile the dicta of Lord Eldon and Lord Cottenham which at first sight seem to conflict.

The petition in this case was from the father of three minor children, and it prayed that they might be delivered up to him by the trustees of his marriage settlement, and that, if necessary, a writ of *habeas corpus* might issue for that purpose. The infants had been taken away by their mother who was living with them out of the jurisdiction of the court, and she had been accompanied by her brother, who was one of the trustees, during part of her journey; and it was alleged, that he and his co-trustee were acquainted with the place of her concealment. On the other side it was alleged, that the father wished to have possession of the children, in order that he might bring them up in the doctrines of the Roman Catholic church, although the mother was a Protestant; and that ever since their marriage she had received from him harsh and unfeeling treatment.

(*g*) See *supra*, p. 54.

Upon this Lord Cottenham observed, that it does not follow, that because a husband's conduct is such as to make his wife unhappy, he is therefore to be deprived of the custody of his children.   To justify such an interference with the father's rights, his misconduct must appear to be of such a nature as to be likely to contaminate and corrupt the morals of his children, as in the *Wellesley case* (*h*).   His Lordship, however, refused to grant the prayer of the petition, on the ground that the infants were not in the custody of the trustees; and as to the alleged knowledge of the brother, he said, " as to compelling him to disclose the place of their concealment, he is a mere witness to that.   I could exercise the jurisdiction of the court over him if he had the children in his custody; but I cannot put it in force against parties to compel them to disclose facts of which they are mere witnesses."

§ 80. But, regard being had to the nature of the cases, where, in order that the court may interfere with effect, it has been held to be necessary that the infant should be entitled to some property, the expedient has been sometimes resorted to of settling a small sum of money upon him, and then filing a bill for the due administration of the property (*i*).   For when the court

(*h*) 2 Russ. 1.   *Supra*, p. 23.

(*i*) It seems that 100*l.* would be sufficient for this purpose. See Macpherson on Infants, Part 1, p. 103, 104.

has once got hold of the case, it will take care
that the interests of the minor are attended to as
regards its custody and education, as well as the
management of its estate. And where there is
no suit, but merely a petition for that purpose,
the Court of Chancery will, in such a case, appoint
a guardian both for the person and for the estate,
although if there is a suit pending it will appoint
a guardian for the *person only* (*k*). Unlike the
case of joint testamentary guardianship, where
the office, as has been previously mentioned, sur-
vives, if several guardians are appointed by the
Court of Chancery, the office determines on the
death of any one of them, although the survivor
or survivors will be re-appointed without a reference to the Master (*l*).

§ 81. Where a testator had left to infants who
were his natural daughters considerable fortunes,
and the Master had appointed a guardian for
them with an allowance for their maintenance,
the mother who was desirous that they should
live with her, presented a petition objecting to
the Master's report and praying that it might be
reviewed. The Lord Chancellor, however, confirmed the appointment of the guardian, but
directed the Master to consider what intercourse

(*k*) Seton's Decrees, 277, 278. *Ex parte Becher*, 1 Bro. C. C.
555.

(*l*) *Bradshaw* v. *Bradshaw*, 1 Russ. 528. *Hall* v. *Jones*, 2
Sim. 41.

between the infants and the mother could be reasonably provided for in the plan of their maintenance and education under the guardian (*m*).   And in the case of an infant of the age of fifteen years, whose father was dead, and with respect to whose custody differences existed between the paternal and maternal relations, the Vice Chancellor of England said, that as the parties could not agree amongst themselves, he considered it to be a matter of course to direct a reference to the Master to approve of a guardian (*n*).

§ 82.   Whatever difficulties may have formerly occurred in questions of guardianship on account of the penal or disabling laws then in force against Roman Catholics, they can hardly be said to exist at the present day (*o*).   Even in the time of Lord Eldon, he admitted that with reference to the distinction between Protestants and Catholics, the court used to interfere in the education of children in many instances in which it would not interfere now (*p*).   And the following im-

(*m*) *Courtois* v. *Vincent*, Reg. Lib. (A), 1820, fol. 303 ; Jac. 268.

(*n*) *Coham* v. *Coham*, 13 Sim. 639.

(*o*) On this subject, see the case of *Lady Teynham*, 4 Bro. Par. Ca. 302.   *Hill* v. *Filkin*, 2 P. Wms. 5.   *Blake* v. *Leigh*, Amb. 306. *In re Bishop*, Reg. Lib. 1774, (A), p. 185 ; Macpherson on Infants, Chap. 12.

(*p*) *Wellesley* v. *Duke of Beaufort*, 2 Russ. 22.   See also as regards dissenters, *per* Lord Cottenham, L. C., in *Knott* v. *Cottee*, 2 Phill. 195.

portant case shows that the court will give the fullest effect to the intention of a Roman Catholic father that his children should be brought up in the tenets of that religion.

G. H. Talbot, who was a Roman Catholic, had married A. Berkeley, a Protestant, and they had issue two children, John and Augusta Talbot. No stipulation had been made in the marriage settlement or otherwise as to the faith in which the children should be educated; but by a separation deed afterwards executed between Mr. and Mrs. Talbot, it was stipulated that the daughter Augusta should, until she attained her tenth year, remain under the sole care and management of her mother, and that the son John should remain with his father, but that the mother should have the liberty of seeing him at all reasonable times. The father died in 1839, having by will appointed the Rev. T. Doyle, a Roman Catholic clergyman, the sole and entire guardian of his children, who were both minors, and his sole executor; and he bequeathed to him the whole of his personal property (q).

The infants were entitled under the will of Charles Earl of Shrewsbury each to a large sum of money, contingently upon their attaining the age of twenty-one years, or in the case of the daughter being married, with a right to allowance during their minorities; and in default of

(q) *Talbot* v. *Earl of Shrewsbury*, 4 Myl. & Cr. 673.

their attaining a vested interest in those sums, John Earl of Shrewsbury, the residuary legatee of Charles Earl of Shrewsbury, would be entitled to the money.

Two suits were instituted for the purpose of having the trusts of the will of Charles Earl of Shrewsbury performed under the decree of the court.

In 1839, after the father's death, a petition was presented in one of the suits to the Lord Chancellor (Lord Cottenham) in the name of the infants, praying that John Earl of Shrewsbury and Doyle might be restrained from taking them or either of them out of the jurisdiction, and that the infants might be permitted to reside with their mother at such reasonable and proper times as to the court should seem meet; and more particularly that the infant John might be permitted to visit and reside with his mother. The petition also prayed that it might be referred to the Master to settle a scheme for the future education of the infants (the son being then nine and the daughter eight years old), regard being had to the just claims of the infants to visit their mother, and reside with her at all convenient times.

At the same time another petition was presented in the other suit by Doyle in the name of the infants, praying, amongst other things, that the infant, John Talbot, might be allowed to reside with the Earl of Shrewsbury and be educated under his inspection but under the direction of Doyle, and also travel abroad with the Earl of Shrewsbury, accompanied by his tutor.

About this time the mother married the Hon. C. F. Berkeley, and various other proceedings took place, until the matter came finally before the court upon a petition presented by Doyle praying that Mr. and Mrs. Berkeley might be ordered to deliver up the person of the infant Augusta Talbot to him as her sole testamentary guardian; and also upon another petition presented by Mrs. Berkeley praying, amongst other things, that her son, John, might have unrestrained intercourse with her and be allowed to visit her at her own residence, and reside with her at convenient and proper times. This petition also alleged, that the Earl of Shrewsbury and Doyle, under whose exclusive power and control the minor son was then placed, were bound by the obligations of conscience as Roman Catholics, and were fully determined, to educate him in the religious tenets of the church of Rome.

We have previously noticed what was said by the court on this occasion with respect to the *rights* of the testamentary guardian as against the mother (*r*); but, under the particular circumstances of the case, it did not think the removal of the daughter Augusta then expedient.

(*r*) *Supra*, p. 115.

With regard to the latter petition, the Lord
Chancellor said, that the court would not, without a case made, interfere with the manner
in which the testamentary guardian exercised
his authority. *Primâ facie*, he had a right to
the possession of both children. He had a right
to exercise his discretion. He had exercised his
discretion for the present, and thought it more
for the benefit of the child that he should be
removed from school, and placed in the house of
his uncle. Then the question was, whether that
peculiar circumstance which had been the subject
of so much discussion was to regulate the mode
of the boy's religious education. It was said
there were circumstances of pecuniary benefit
and property which ought to induce the court
to educate him in a manner which, if it were the
duty of the court to interfere, it would find it
very difficult to prescribe. In the first place,
this child was born of a Roman Catholic father,
who, though he married a Protestant lady, did
not, on that marriage, enter into any stipulation
as to the faith in which his children should be
brought up. The father, who had the power of
regulating the method of bringing up his children, and of extending that power after his death,
appointed, as testamentary guardian, a clergyman of the Roman Catholic church, and the
court thought it impossible that the father could

more distinctly indicate his wishes as to the faith in which his child should be brought up. Although the father has not the power of regulating, after his death, the faith in which his child should be brought up, the court will pay great attention to the expression of his wishes, and he can exercise that power indirectly by appointing a guardian of that faith. When, therefore, a Roman Catholic father appoints a Roman Catholic guardian, there can be no doubt as to the father's intention; and if the court were to interfere with the exercise of the guardian's discretion as to the faith in which the child should be educated, it would be doing an act of very great injustice. Nothing can be more dear to a father than regulating the religious education of his child; and if the court were to interfere in the manner desired, it would adopt a course to induce those dissenting from the Established Church to suppose that the court would interfere to control the education of their children. The Lord Chancellor then alluded to the observations of Lord Eldon, in the case of *Wellesley* v. *Duke of Beaufort* (*s*), upon which he remarked: he says, " that the law is now changed, and that it is now lawful to educate a child in the Roman Catholic faith; and when he speaks

(*s*) 2 Russ. 21. *Supra*, p. 129. See also *In re North*, 11 Jur. 7, and *supra*, p. 36. 52.

of former times he speaks of times when the vain attempt was made to influence the religion of families by penal statutes."

The petition was therefore dismissed.

§ 83. It is in order that the court may be able to exercise its superintending care over infants with effect, that it has always shown great jealousy in allowing infants over whom it has control to be taken out of its jurisdiction by going abroad.

We have seen that even a father, who was an alien, has, under particular circumstances, been restrained from removing his minor child to a foreign country (t); and where permission has been given to him to carry his children, who were wards of court, abroad with him, a special undertaking has been required that he would bring them back with him on his return, and in the meantime inform the court, by proper vouchers half-yearly, of the plan of education pursued with regard to each of the children, and specify where and with whom they resided (u). In *Campbell* v. *Mackay* (v), Lord Cottenham, with reference to this question, said, "Independently of this well established rule of the court, and the principle

(t) *De Manneville* v. *De Manneville*, 10 Ves. 52. *Supra*, p. 20. 22.

(u) *Anon.* Jac. 264, n. (a). *Supra*, p. 50, 51. See also *Stephens* v. *James*, 1 M. & Keen, 627. *Lethem* v. *Hall*, 7 Sim. 141.

(v) 2 Myl. & Cr. 31.

upon which it proceeds, I am convinced that scarcely anything can be more injurious to the future prospects of English children and particularly of English boys, than a permanent residence abroad. Without the proper opportunities of attending the religious service of the church to which they belong, separated from their natural connections, estranged from the members of their own families, withdrawn from the courses of education which their contemporaries are pursuing, and accutomed to habits and manners which are not those of their own country, they must be becoming from day to day, less and less adapted to the position which it is to be wished they should hereafter occupy in their native land."

CHAPTER VIII.

CUSTODY OF INFANTS UNDER STAT. 2 & 3 VICT. CAP. 54.

§ 84. THE hardships, not to say cruelty, inflicted upon unoffending mothers by a state of the law which took such little account of their claims or feelings, in a matter in which they are so deeply interested as the custody of their own children, had for a long time attracted attention before a partial remedy was provided; and it was not without much difficulty, and after much opposition, that in 1839, the statute was passed which forms the subject of the present chapter, and which is generally known by the name of Mr. Justice Talfourd's Act.

When the bill was in the House of Lords, Lord Lyndhurst gave it his powerful support, and thus described the evils which it was intended in some degree to remedy (*a*). He said, that by the law of England, as it then stood, the father had an absolute right to the custody of his children, and to take them from the mother. However pure might be her conduct—however amiable—how-

(*a*) Hansard's Parl. Deb. vol. 49, p. 436 (3rd series).

ever correct in all the relations of life, the father might, if he thought proper, exclude her from all access to the children, and might do this from the most corrupt motives. He might be a man of the most profligate habits; for the purpose of extorting money, or in order to induce her to concede to his profligate conduct, he might exclude her from all access to their common children, and the course of the law would afford her no redress. That was the state of the law as it then existed. Need he say, that it was a cruel law—that it was unnatural—that it was tyrannous—that it was unjust?

On the other side it was argued, that the father was responsible for the rearing up of the child; but when unhappy differences separated the father and mother, to give the custody of the child to the father, and to allow access to it by the mother, was to injure the child; for it was natural to expect that the mother would not instil into the latter any respect for the husband whom she might hate or despise. Such a system would prevent a child from being properly brought up. The present Lord Chancellor rested his opposition to the bill, chiefly on the ground that it did not sufficiently attend to the conservation of the rights of the children, and he thought that objections existed to the machinery of the first two clauses which must render it impossible to adopt the bill.

§ 85. This statute enacts,—

I. That it shall be lawful for the Lord Chancellor and the Master of the Rolls in England, and for the Lord Chancellor and the Master of the Rolls in Ireland, respectively, upon hearing the petition of the mother of any infant or infants being in the sole custody or control of the father thereof, or of any person by his authority, or of any guardian after the death of the father, if he shall see fit, to make order for the access of the petitioner to such infant or infants, at such times and subject to such regulations as he shall deem convenient and just; and if such infant or infants shall be within the age of seven years, to make order that such infant or infants shall be delivered to and remain in the custody of the petitioner until attaining such age, subject to such regulations as he shall deem convenient and just.

II. That on all complaints made under this act, it shall be lawful for the Lord Chancellor or the Master of the Rolls in England, and for the Lord Chancellor or the Master of the Rolls in Ireland, to receive affidavits sworn before any Master in ordinary or Master extraordinary of the Court of Chancery; and that any person who shall depose falsely and corruptly in any affidavits so sworn shall be deemed guilty of perjury, and incur the penalties thereof.

III. That all orders which shall be made by virtue of this act by the Lord Chancellor or the

Master of the Rolls in England, and by the Lord Chancellor or the Master of the Rolls in Ireland, shall be enforced by process of contempt of the High Court of Chancery in England and Ireland respectively.

IV. Provided always, That no order shall be made by virtue of this act whereby any mother against whom adultery shall be established, by judgment in an action for criminal conversation at the suit of her husband, or by the sentence of an Ecclesiastical Court, shall have the custody of any infant or access to any infant, anything herein contained to the contrary notwithstanding.

§ 86. Although this act in terms mentions only the Lord Chancellor and the Master of the Rolls, yet under it, the Vice Chancellors have equally jurisdiction (b). Indeed, it has been said by authority, that when the bill was introduced into the House of Lords, it did contain the words "the Vice Chancellor;" but those words were struck out because, jurisdiction being expressly given to the Lord Chancellor, that jurisdiction could be exercised by the Vice Chancellor as a matter of course, and therefore it was deemed unnecessary to mention him (c).

§ 87. Soon after the passing of the act, a peti-

(b) *In re Taylor*, 10 Sim. 291.
(c) Ib. 292.

tion was presented to the Vice Chancellor (of England) by Mrs. Taylor (*d*), living apart from her husband, who had taken their five children, two of whom were more than seven years old, but the other three under that age, to reside with him in France; and she prayed that such of the children of the marriage as were under the age of seven years might be delivered to and remain with her until they attained that age; and that she might be at liberty to have access to such of the children as the court might not order her to have the custody of, under such regulations as to the court might deem right.

It appeared that Mrs. Taylor had quitted her husband's house on suspicion of his having committed adultery; but she afterwards admitted that she was mistaken, and that this charge against him was wholly without foundation. They, however, remained separate for a considerable period, and at last Mrs. Taylor instituted a suit for the restitution of conjugal rights. This suit was pending when the petition came on for hearing before the Vice Chancellor.

On the part of Mr. Taylor, it was contended that the act, 2 & 3 Vict. c. 54, left the legal right of the father exactly as it was previously; it established no new jurisdiction, but enlarged that which already existed, leaving the character

(*d*) *In re Taylor*, 11 Sim. 178.

of the enlarged jurisdiction as it found it, merely
discretionary; and that it was never meant to
apply to the case of children resident out of the
jurisdiction, where such residence had commenced
before proceedings under the act were taken;
much less could it be applicable, when the sub-
ject-matter was situate in a foreign country,
governed by independent laws, and not subject
to the British Crown.

The Vice Chancellor (of England) in giving
judgment said, that as the jurisdiction given by
the act was to be exercised solely in the discretion of the court, it would be hardly right for
the court to say that the lady was entitled to
have access to her children, pending the question
in the Ecclesiastical Court which she had thought
proper to raise. He thought that the conduct
of the husband had been *bonâ fide* throughout.
He refused, therefore, to make any order on the
petition, until he knew the result of the proceedings in the Ecclesiastical Court, and the petition
was to stand over with liberty to apply.

§ 88. The question of jurisdiction under this
statute came also recently under the consideration
of Vice Chancellor Knight Bruce, in a case where
a petition was presented by a Mrs. Tomlinson,
praying that her infant son, not quite two years
old, might be delivered into her custody, subject

to such regulations as the court might think fit
to make. She had been married in 1845, and
the child was born in March, 1847, but the husband and wife had lived separate since July, 1846,
she charging him with acts of cruelty towards
her. In November, 1848, the husband instituted
a suit in the Consistory Court of Chester for the
restitution of conjugal rights, and. on the 5th of
March, 1849, he sued out a writ of *habeas corpus*,
returnable before Mr. Justice Patteson, to get
possession of his child. The case was however
adjourned by the learned Judge until the 27th
of March, in consequence of the wife alleging that
she was about to apply by petition to the Court
of Chancery, and in the meantime bail was taken
for the production of the infant.

It was objected before the Vice Chancellor,
that the case was not within the stat. 2 & 3 Vict.
c. 54, which applied only where the infant was
" in the sole custody or control of the father
thereof, or of any person by his authority." His
Honor, however, said, that he thought that the
court, upon the equity of the statute had jurisdiction. Judging from admitted facts, he was
of opinion, that there was no reasonable probability that the mother would succeed in her
resistance to the suit instituted by her husband,
but as she wished to file further affidavits which,
under the circumstances of the case, seemed to

be allowable, his Honor ordered the petition to
stand over until further order to be made within
a time specified; and directed that in the meantime, as the infant was a weakly child, and then
under good care and in a state of comfort and
security, it should remain where it was—the
mother and the next friend undertaking to make
proper provision for its maintenance and care.

Upon this, an application was made on the
part of the father, for an order that he might
have access to the infant in the meantime; but
the Vice Chancellor said, " No ; I have thought
of that; but on the whole, I do not feel inclined
to grant it" (e).

§ 89. The case of *Warde* v. *Warde* (*f*), has been
previously cited, and the facts have been detailed,
so far as they were necessary to show the kind
of conduct on the part of a father against which
the Court of Chancery will interfere for the protection of infants.   The petition of Mrs. Warde
was intituled both in the cause and in the matter
of the Custody of Infants' Act, 2 & 3 Vict. c. 54,

(e) The petition was heard and the original order made, March
31st, 1849.   The parties afterwards agreed to live together, and
no further application was made to the court.

(*f*) *Supra*, p. 31—36.   It is there stated that the case has not
been reported, but this is a mistake.   It will be found in 2 Phill.
786, although the judgment, as to the effect of the evidence, is
not so fully there given as in the text, *ubi supra*.

and the Lord Chancellor having suggested that it should stand over, in the hope that some amicable arrangement might be come to by the parties, said, that the object of the act and of the promoters of it, and that which he thought appeared on the face of the act itself, was to protect mothers from the tyranny of those husbands who ill-used them. Unfortunately, as the law stood before, however much a woman might have been injured, she was precluded from seeking justice from her husband by the terror of that power which the law gave to him of taking her children from her. That was felt to be so great a hardship and injustice, that Parliament thought the mother ought to have the protection of the law with respect to her children up to a certain age, and that she should be at liberty to assert her rights as a wife, without the risk of any injury being done to her feelings as a mother. That was the object with which the act was introduced, and that was the construction he put upon it. It gave the court the power of interfering, and when the court saw that the maternal feelings were tortured for the purpose of obtaining anything like an unjust advantage over the mother, that was precisely the case in which it would be called upon and ought to interfere.

The result was that, as has been already men-

tioned, the Lord Chancellor made an order for
the removal of all the children from the custody
of the father, and their delivery to the mother,
she and her brother undertaking to maintain
them until further order.   At the same time, as
was the case in *Shelley* v. *Westbrooke* (*g*), the
father was restrained from applying for a writ
of *habeas corpus;* for otherwise, as the Lord
Chancellor observed, the order might be reversed
by a Judge at common law.

§ 90. It may be useful to mention that by
stat. 3 & 4 Vict. c. 90, the following provisions
have been enacted with respect to the care and
custody of infants, who have been convicted of
felony.

Sect. 1, provides, That in every case in which
any person being under the age of twenty-one
years shall hereafter be convicted of felony, it
shall be lawful for her Majesty's High Court of
Chancery, upon the application of any person or
persons who may be willing to take charge of
such infant, and to provide for his or her maintenance and education, if such court shall find
that the same will be for the benefit of such
infant, due regard being had to the age of the
infant, and to the circumstances, habits, and
character of the parents, testamentary or natural

(*g*) 1 Jac. 265. *Supra,* p. 36.

guardian, of such infant, to assign the care and custody of such infant, during his or her minority, or any part thereof, to such person or persons, upon such terms and conditions, and subject to such regulations respecting the maintenance, education, and care of such infant, as the said Court of Chancery shall think proper to prescribe and direct; and upon any order for that purpose being made, and so long as the same shall remain in force, the same shall be binding and obligatory upon the father, and upon every testamentary or natural guardian of such infant, and no person or persons shall be entitled to use or exercise any power or control over such infant which may be inconsistent with such order of the said Court of Chancery: Provided always, That the said court may at any time rescind such assignment, or from time to time rescind, alter, or vary any such terms or conditions, or such regulations, as to the said court may seem fit; and provided also, that the said High Court of Chancery shall and may award such costs as to it may seem fit, against any such person or persons who shall make such application as aforesaid, if such application shall not appear to the said court well founded, and such costs shall be payable to any parent, or other natural or testamentary guardian of any such child who shall oppose such application.

Sect. 2, enacts, That in every case it shall be a part of the terms and conditions upon which such care and custody shall be assigned, that the infant shall not, during the period of such care and custody, be sent beyond the seas or out of the jurisdiction of the said Court of Chancery.

APPENDIX.

———◆———

ORDER IN COURT OF CHANCERY FOR HABEAS CORPUS FOR
DELIVERY OF CHILDREN TO FATHER (a).

The Order was made on Petition.

His Lordship doth order that a writ of *habeas corpus*
do issue, returnable immediately, directed to the said
Emily Mary Marchioness of Salisbury, and Emily Anne
Bennett Elizabeth Countess of Westmeath, to bring
before his Lordship the bodies of Lord Delvin and Lady
Rosa Nugent, at his Lordship's room, on Saturday
morning the 19th instant, at eleven o'clock. In the
matter of the children of the Earl of Westmeath, L. C.,
16th June, 1819.   Reg. Lib. (A), 1818, fol. 1359.

ORDER ON HABEAS CORPUS FOR DELIVERY OF CHILDREN
TO FATHER.

His Lordship doth order that the bodies of the said
Lord Delvin and Lady Rosa Nugent, the children of
the said Earl of Westmeath, be delivered to him.   In the
matter of the children of Earl of Westmeath, L. C., 23rd
June, 1819.   Reg. Lib. (A), 1818, fol. 1534.   S. C.
Jac. 251, note.

(a) See Seton's Decrees and Orders in Equity, p. 281.

ORDER IN COURT OF CHANCERY FOR HABEAS CORPUS FOR BRINGING UP CHILDREN ON APPLICATION OF FATHER.

The Order was made on Motion.

HIS Lordship doth order that a writ of *habeas corpus* do issue, directing the said defendants George Blenkin and Mary his wife, to bring into this court the plaintiffs Mary Lyons, Frances Lyons, and Jane Beatson Lyons, the infant children of the said John Lyons, at the sitting of this court, at Westminster Hall, on the 10th of February next. *Lyons* v. *Blenkin*, L. C., 15th January, 1820. Reg. Lib. (B), 1819, fol. 208. S. C. Jac. 247. *Supra*, p. 37.

WRIT OF HABEAS CORPUS IN THE ABOVE CASE (*b*).

GEORGE THE THIRD, &c. To George Blenkin and Mary his wife greeting. We command you, that you do on Thursday, the 15th day of February next, bring before us in our Court of Chancery, at the sitting thereof at Westminster Hall, the bodies of Mary Lyons, Frances Lyons, and Jane Beatson Lyons, or by whatsoever name or addition they are known or called, who are detained in custody, to perform and abide such order as our said court shall make in their behalf. And hereof fail not, and bring this writ with you. Witness ourself, at Westminster, the 29th day of January, in the sixtieth year of our reign.

(*b*) The question of whether a writ in this form issues from the equity or common law side of the Court of Chancery, has very recently been fully discussed before the Judicial Committee of the Privy Council, in a case *In re Belson*, (Jan. 24th, 1850), in which judgment has not yet been given.

THE within named George Blenkin and Mary his wife do hereby certify to the Right Honorable the Lord High Chancellor of Great Britain, that the within-named plaintiffs Mary Lyons, Frances Lyons, and Jane Beatson Lyons, are detained by and are under the protection of the said Mary Blenkin, in the parish of Sculcoates in the county of York, for the purpose of being educated and maintained by her as their guardian, under the will of their grandmother, Mary Beatson, deceased, and according to the trusts and directions for those purposes contained in the said will. Dated the 9th of February, 1820.

ORDER FOR GUARDIAN AND MAINTENANCE ON PETITION.

IT is ordered, that it be referred to Mr. S., one, &c., to approve of a proper person or persons to be appointed guardian or guardians of the person and estate of the petitioner during her minority. And it is ordered, that all proper parties have notice to attend the said Master thereon, and be at liberty to propose such guardian or guardians. And it is ordered, that the said Master do inquire and state the petitioner's age, and the nature and amount of her fortune, and what relations she has, and on what evidence or ground he approves of such person or persons so to be appointed guardian or guardians. And it is ordered, that the said Master do inquire and state what will be proper to be allowed for the maintenance and education of the petitioner during her minority, and from what past period such allowance should commence, and out of what fund it should be taken. And after the said Master shall have made his report, such further order shall be made as shall be just. In the matter of Arnold, M. R., 1st December, 1814. Reg. Lib. (A), 1814, fol. 50.

ORDER FOR LIBERTY TO TAKE INFANTS ABROAD.

His Lordship doth order that the petitioner, as the father of the said infants, plaintiffs, be at liberty to remove the said infants, plaintiffs, with him to America aforesaid, or to such other parts and places beyond the seas, and out of the jurisdiction of this court, in which he shall in the execution of his duty be ordered to find it necessary to reside, there to remain with the petitioner in case the petitioner shall so think fit; the petitioner, by his said petition, undertaking to bring the said infants, plaintiffs, or such of them as shall then be living, back with him, on his return to this country on the fulfilment of his mission in the petition mentioned, unless the petitioner shall in the meantime, from any unforeseen circumstance deem it advisable to send them, or any of them back to this country. But the petitioner is half-yearly to transmit, properly vouched, to be laid before the court, the plan of tuition and education for each of the said infants actually adopted and in practice at the time of such half-yearly return, and specifying particularly where and with whom they reside. *Jackson* v. *Hankey*, L. C., 15th May, 1823. Reg. Lib. (A), 1822, fol. 1088. S. C. Jac. 265. *Supra*, p. 50, 51.

INDEX.

FATHER—*continued.*

in England, 10, 11.

statement of cases of exception to his right, 13. 23. 26.
36, 37. 52. 70.

where there has been with his consent a partial enjoy-
ment by infant of pecuniary benefit, 39—48. 50.

respect paid by Court of Chancery to his wishes, 111. 122.

mere fact of his insolvency no ground for depriving him
of the custody of his children, 37, 38.

Courts of Common Law will interfere to protect child
from injury by, 62, 63. 65.

general misconduct of, 75. 127.

FELONS,

custody of infant felons under stat. 3 & 4 Vict. c. 90—
146.

FORCE,

father may not commit breach of peace to get possession
of his child, 88.

distinction between case of father and a stranger where
force used, 87. 91, 92.

FRANCE.   See CODE CIVIL.

FRAUD,

vitiates claim to custody in case of illegitimate child,
89, 90.

GUARDIANSHIP,

different kinds of guardianship, 107.

where mother of infant guardian for nurture, 108.

where mother natural guardian of infant, 109.

of infants properly a trust, 27. 121.

appointment of testamentary guardian under 12 Car. 2,
c. 24—109, 110.

father alone can appoint testamentary guardian, 111.

respect paid by courts to wishes of father, 111. 122.

rights of testamentary guardian, 74. 111. 115. 119.
122.

he stands *in loco patris*, 111.

he cannot be removed without bill, 119. See 117, n. (*v*).

THE END.

LONDON:
RAYNER AND HODGES, PRINTERS,
109, Fetter Lane, Fleet Street.

Catalogue of Law Books

PUBLISHED BY

WILLIAM BENNING AND C⁰.,

LAW BOOKSELLERS,

43, *FLEET STREET, LONDON.*

CONTENTS.

PRACTICE, PLEADING, ETC., AT COMMON LAW.

ROSCOE'S EVIDENCE AT NISI PRIUS.

A DIGEST of the LAW of EVIDENCE on the TRIAL of ACTIONS at NISI PRIUS. By Henry Roscoe, Esq., of the Inner Temple, Barrister at Law. Seventh Edition, with considerable additions. By Edward Smirke, Esq., Barrister at Law. *In royal 12mo.* (1849.) *Price 1l. 4s. boards.*

LLOYD ON PROHIBITION.

A TREATISE on the LAW of PROHIBITION, containing a concise View of the Principles on which that Writ is granted, and also the Practice of the same, together with an Appendix containing a collection of Points decided on Applications for Prohibitions to the new County Courts. By Morgan Lloyd, Esq., of the Middle Temple, Barrister at Law. *In 12mo.* (1849.) *Price 5s. boards.*

TAPPING ON MANDAMUS.

The LAW and PRACTICE of the High Prerogative WRIT of MANDAMUS, as it obtains both in England and Ireland. By Thomas Tapping, Esq., of the Middle Temple, Barrister at Law. *In royal 8vo.* (1848.) *Price 1l. 1s. boards.*

SMITH'S SUIT AT LAW.

An ELEMENTARY VIEW of the PROCEEDINGS in an ACTION at LAW. By the late J. W. Smith, Esq., Barrister at Law. Third Edition, with Additions and Notes. By David Babington Ring, Esq., B.A., of the Middle Temple, Barrister at Law. *Third Edition.* 12mo. (1848.) *Price 7s. 6d. boards.*

LETTERS ON SPECIAL PLEADING.

POPULAR LETTERS on SPECIAL PLEADING, addressed to those about to enter on the Study of the Common Law. By Joseph Philips, Esq., M. A., Special Pleader. *In 8vo. Price 2s. 6d. sewed.*

CHITTY (J. JUN.) ON PLEADING.

PRECEDENTS in PLEADING, with copious Notes on Pleading, Practice, and Evidence. By the late Joseph Chitty, Jun., Esq. The Second Edition, containing References to all the Cases decided upon the New Rules of Pleading, and short preliminary Observations on the more important Subjects. By Henry Pearson, Esq., of the Middle Temple, Barrister at Law.

In 1 vol. royal 8vo. (1847.) Price 2l. boards.

Part II. may be had separately, *price 1l. 1s. boards.*

FELLOWS ON COSTS.

The LAW of COSTS, as affected by the Small Debts' Act and other Statutes, requiring a Judge's certificate where the Damages are under a limited Amount, with various Cases, shewing in what Instances a Plaintiff may still sue in the Superior Courts. By Thomas Howard Fellows, of the Inner Temple.

In 12mo. (1847.) Price 4s. boards.

GILBERT'S TABLE OF COSTS.

BILLS of COSTS between ATTORNEY and AGENT, in the Courts of Queen's Bench, Common Pleas, Exchequer of Pleas, and Crown Office; shewing at one view Sets of Costs complete in themselves: also in Bankruptcy, Insolvency, Chancery, Conveyancing, Privy Council, Replevin, Sci. Fa., &c., with other Miscellaneous Bills, and a Copious Index. By E. W. Gilbert. Third Edition, considerably enlarged. *In 8vo. (1847.) Price 16s. cloth boards.*

SAUNDERS'S REPORTS.

The REPORTS of the most learned Sir EDMUND SAUNDERS, Knt., late Lord Chief Justice of the King's Bench, of several Pleadings and Cases in the Court of King's Bench, in the time of the Reign of his most excellent Majesty King Charles the Second. Edited, with Notes and References to the Pleadings and Cases, by John Williams, one of his late Majesty's Serjeants at Law. The Fifth Edition, by John Patteson, of the Middle Temple, Esq., now one of the Judges of the Court of Queen's Bench, and Edward Vaughan Williams, of Lincoln's Inn, Esq., Barrister-at-Law. Sixth Edition, by Edward Vaughan Williams, Esq. (now one of the Judges of the Court of Common Pleas.)

In 3 vols, royal 8vo. (1845.) Price 4l. 4s. boards.

MACNAMARA ON COUNTS AND PLEAS.

A PRACTICAL TREATISE on the Several COUNTS and PLEAS allowed to be pleaded together in CIVIL PROCEEDINGS, under the Statute 4 Anne, c. 16, and the New Rules of Hilary Term, 4 Wm. 4, and other Rules and Statutes. By Henry Macnamara, Esq., of Lincoln's Inn, Special Pleader.

In 12mo. (1844.) Price 5s. boards.

HARRISON'S ANALYTICAL DIGEST.

A DIGEST of all the REPORTED CASES determined in the HOUSE of LORDS, the several Courts of Common Law in Banc, and at Nisi Prius, and the Court of Bankruptcy, from 1756 to 1843; including also the Crown Cases reserved, and a full Selection of Equity Decisions, with the MS. Cases cited in the best Modern Treatises, not elsewhere reported. By R. Tarrant Harrison, Esq., of the Middle Temple. *Third Edition. Royal 8vo.* (1844.) 4 *thick vols. Price 6l. 16s. 6d. boards.*

PHILLIPPS'S LAW OF EVIDENCE.

A TREATISE on the LAW of EVIDENCE. Ninth Edition, with considerable Alterations and Additions. By S. M. Phillipps, Esq.
In 2 vols. royal 8vo. (1843.) *Price 2l. 10s. boards.*

STEPHEN (MR SERJT.) ON PLEADING.

A TREATISE on the PRINCIPLES of PLEADING in CIVIL ACTIONS; comprising a summary View of the whole Proceedings in a Suit at Law. By Henry John Stephen, Serjeant at Law. The Fifth Edition, with great Additions.
In 8vo. (1843.) *Price 18s. boards.*

WALFORD ON PARTIES TO ACTIONS.

A TREATISE on the LAW respecting PARTIES to ACTIONS. By Frederic Walford, Esq., Special Pleader. *In 2 vols,* 12mo. (1842.) *Price 1l. 10s. bds.*

LUTWYCHE ON PLEADING.

An INQUIRY into the Principles of PLEADING the GENERAL ISSUE, since the Promulgation of the NEW RULES, 4 Wm. 4, and of Trinity Term, 1 Victoria, with a Supplement, containing the Cases on the Effect of the General Issue to Trinity Term, 1842. By Alfred J. P. Lutwyche, M.A.
In 12mo. (1842). *Price 7s. 6d. boards.*

CAREY'S BOROUGH COURT RULES.

BOROUGH COURT RULES, 2 & 3 Vict. c. 27, with an Appendix of Statutes, &c. By Peter Stafford Carey, Esq. *In royal 8vo.* (1841.) *Price 5s. boards.*

ARCHBOLD'S PLEADING AND EVIDENCE.

A DIGEST of the LAW relative to PLEADING and EVIDENCE in CIVIL ACTIONS. Second Edition. By J. F. Archbold, Esq., Barrister at Law.
In 12mo. (1837.) *Price 16s. boards.*

MANNING'S EXCHEQUER PRACTICE.

The PRACTICE of the COURT of EXCHEQUER, (Revenue Branch). By James Manning, Serjeant at Law. The Second Edition corrected and enlarged, with an Appendix, containing an Inquiry into the Tenure of the Conventionary Estates in the Assessionable Manors, Parcel of the Duchy of Cornwall.
In royal 8vo. (1837.) *Price 1l. 11s. 6d. boards.*

HENNELL'S FORMS OF DECLARATIONS.

FORMS of DECLARATIONS in Common Assumpsit and Debt on Simple Contract, &c., prepared in Conformity with the General Rules of Trinity Term, 4 Wm. 4, with Practical Notes and Directions. By Charles Hennell, Esq., Special Pleader. *Second Edition. In 8vo.* (1837.) *Price 12s. boards.*

GIBBONS ON LIMITATION.

LEX TEMPORIS, a Treatise on the Law of Limitation and Prescription. By D. Gibbons, Esq., Special Pleader. *In 12mo.* (1835.) *Price 7s. boards.*

PRACTICE, PLEADING, ETC., IN EQUITY.

ADAMS ON THE DOCTRINE OF EQUITY.
DOCTRINE of EQUITY; a Commentary on the Law as administered by the Court of Chancery; being the Substance (with Additions) of Three Series of Lectures delivered before the Incorporated Law Society, in the Years 1842—5. By the late John Adams, Junr., Esq., Barrister at Law. (1849.)

FORMS OF WRITS IN CHANCERY.
FORMS of WRITS and other PROCEEDINGS on the Common Law side of the Court of Chancery, issuing out of and heretofore prepared in the Petty Bag Office. By F. G. Abbott, Clerk of the Petty Bag. (1849.) *Price 3s. 6d. boards.*

PETTY BAG OFFICE.
GENERAL RULES and ORDERS of the HIGH COURT OF CHANCERY, of the Common Law Side thereof, as to Proceedings in the Petty Bag Office. (By authority.) (1849.) *Price 1s.*

BATTEN ON CONTRACTS.
A PRACTICAL TREATISE on the LAW relating to the Specific Performance of CONTRACTS. By Edmund Batten, Esq., Barrister at Law.
In 8vo. (1849.) *Price 14s. boards.*

GOLDSMITH'S EQUITY.
The DOCTRINE and PRACTICE of EQUITY; or a Concise Outline of Proceedings in the High Court of Chancery; designed principally for the Use of Students. By G. Goldsmith, A.M., Barrister at Law. According to the last New Orders. *Fourth Edition, in 8vo.* (1849.) *Price 14s. boards.*

EQUITY PRECEDENTS.
EQUITY PRECEDENTS, comprising BILLS, PETITIONS, and ANSWERS, adapted to the Orders of May, 1845; with Notes on Pleading and Evidence. By Robert Whitworth, Esq., M.A., Barrister at Law. *In 8vo.* (1848.) *1l. 2s. bds.*

SMITH'S HANDBOOK IN CHANCERY.
A HANDBOOK of the PRACTICE of the COURT of CHANCERY, adapted to the Orders of the 8th of May, 1845, and the Decisions thereon. By John Sidney Smith, Esq., Barrister at Law. *In 8vo.* (1848.) *Price 1l. 2s. boards.*

CALVERT'S PARTIES TO SUITS IN EQUITY.
A TREATISE on the LAW respecting PARTIES to SUITS in EQUITY. Second Edition. By Frederick Calvert, Esq., of the Inner Temple, Barrister at Law, Fellow of Merton College, Oxford. *In royal 8vo.* (1847.) *1l. 1s. bds.*

GRESLEY ON EVIDENCE.
A TREATISE on the LAW of EVIDENCE in the COURTS of EQUITY. By the late Richard Newcombe Gresley, Esq., M.A., Barrister at Law. Second Edition, with such Alterations and Additions as to render it conformable to the Statutes, Decisions, and General Orders regulating the Law and Practice, as to Evidence in the High Court of Chancery, together with divers Illustrations, by reference to the Law and Practice as to Evidence in the Courts of Common Law and Civil Law. By Christopher Alderson Calvert, Esq., M.A., Barrister at Law. *Second Edition, in royal 8vo.* (1847.) *Price 1l. 8s. boards.*

ACTA CANCELLARIÆ.

ACTA CANCELLARIÆ; or Selections from the Records of the Court of Chancery, remaining in the Office of Reports and Entries. In Two Parts. Part I. containing Extracts from the Masters' Reports and Certificates, during the Reigns of Queen Elizabeth and King James the First. Part II. containing Extracts from the Registrars' Books, from A.D. 1545, to the end of the Reign of Queen Elizabeth. By Cecil Monro, Esq., one of the Registrars of the Court. *In 8vo.* (1847.) *Price 1l. 5s. boards.*

ORDINES CANCELLARIÆ.

ORDINES CANCELLARIÆ, containing the General Orders of the High Court of Chancery, from the year 1814 to the year 1845. By Charles Beavan, Esq., Barrister at Law. *In 12mo.* (1845.) *Price 9s. boards.*

A SUPPLEMENT, containing the Orders from 1842 to 1845, may be had separately. *Price 3s. 6d. sewed.*

HUBBACK ON THE EVIDENCE OF SUCCESSION.

A TREATISE on the EVIDENCE of SUCCESSION to REAL and PERSONAL PROPERTY and PEERAGES. By John Hubback, of the Inner Temple, Esq., Barrister at Law. *In royal 8vo.* (1844.) *Price 1l. 11s. 6d. boards.*

CHAMBERS ON INFANTS.

A PRACTICAL TREATISE on the JURISDICTION of the HIGH COURT of CHANCERY over the PERSONS and PROPERTY of INFANTS. By John David Chambers, M.A., Barrister at Law.
In royal 8vo. (1842.) *Price 1l. 10s. boards.*

STOCK ON LUNACY.

A PRACTICAL TREATISE on the LAW of NON COMPOTES MENTIS, or PERSONS of UNSOUND MIND. By John Shapland Stock, of the Middle Temple, Esq., Barrister at Law. *In 8vo.* (1838.) *Price 12s. boards.*

JEMMETT'S SUGDEN'S ACTS.

SUGDEN'S ACTS. The Acts relating to the Administration of Law in Courts of Equity, passed the Sessions of 1 Wm. 4, 2 Wm. 4, 4 & 5 Wm. 4, and 5 & 6 Wm. 4. With an Introduction and Notes. By William Thomas Jemmett, Esq., of Lincoln's Inn, Barrister at Law. *Second Edition, 12mo.* (1836.) *Price 7s. boards.*

SETON'S DECREES IN EQUITY.

A New Edition (containing the Notes of Sir Henry Seton), by W. Harrison, Esq., of the Inner Temple, Barrister at Law, and Cecil Monro, Esq., a Registrar of the Court of Chancery, is preparing for Publication.

CHITTY'S EQUITY INDEX.

CHITTY's (Edw.) INDEX to all the Reported Cases, Statutes, and General Orders, in or relating to the Principles, Pleading, and Practice of Equity and Bankruptcy, in the several Courts of Equity in England and Ireland, the Privy Council and the House of Lords, from the earliest period down to the present time. *Third Edition, royal 8vo., will be published shortly.*

EDEN ON INJUNCTIONS.

A New Edition. By James Haig, of Lincoln's Inn, Esq., Barrister at Law. Preparing for Publication.

REAL PROPERTY, CONVEYANCING, ETC.

HUSBAND AND WIFE.
A Treatise on the Law of Husband and Wife, so far as respects Property; founded upon the Text of Roper, and comprising all Mr. Jacob's Notes and Additions. By John Edward Bright, Esq., of the Inner Temple, Barrister at Law. *In 2 vols, royal 8vo.* (1849.) *Price 2l. 10s. boards.*

COPYHOLD PRECEDENTS.
A Collection of Copyhold Precedents in Conveyancing, arranged for General and Ordinary Use; together with Introductory Treatises upon the various Transactions and Occurrences incident to Estates of Customary Tenure; and an Appendix of Abstracts of Title, and Extracts from relative Acts of Parliament. By John Fish Stansfield, Esq.
In 8vo. (1849.) *Price 12s. boards.*

MINES OF CORNWALL, &c.
A Treatise on the Law relating to Mines, having reference chiefly to the Mines of Cornwall and Devonshire, and the Rights and Liabilities of Adventurers under the Cost Book System. By R. P. Collier, Esq., Barrister at Law. *In 12mo.* (1849.) *Price 6s. boards.*

STEWART'S CONVEYANCING.
The Practice of Conveyancing, comprising every usual Deed, analytically and synthetically arranged. By James Stewart, of Lincoln's Inn, Esq., Barrister at Law. Third Edition, corrected and enlarged, including select Precedents under the Copyhold Enfranchisement Act, 4 & 5 Vict. c. 35, and the Conveyancing Acts of 1845. By James Stewart, Esq., and Harris Prendergast, Esq., of Lincoln's Inn, Barristers at Law.
In 2 parts. (1846-7.) *Price 2l. 4s. boards.*

> Vol. II. comprising all usual Agreements, Bonds, and Wills, price 1l. 2s. *boards.*
> Vol. III. comprising Rules for the Preparation and Examination of all ordinary Abstracts of Title, together with the Law of Evidence connected with the Title to Real and Personal Property. Second Edition, 1840, price 1l. 2s. *boards.*

AIDS FOR STUDENTS.
Aids for Students of Conveyancing. By F. T. Sergeant, of Lincoln's Inn, Esq., Barrister at Law. *In 8vo.* (1847.) *Price 5s. boards.*

HOBLER'S FAMILIAR EXERCISES.
Familiar Exercises between an Attorney and his Articled Clerk, on the General Principles of the Laws of Real Property, &c. By F. Hobler, Jun., Attorney at Law. *Third Edition. In 12mo.* (1847.) *Price 6s. cloth boards.*

SMITH ON FINES.
A Succinct View of the Operation of Fines and Recoveries, for the Use of Students and those who are engaged in the Investigation of Titles, with the Fines and Recoveries Act, and the subsequent Enactments, Orders, and Decisions relating thereto. By Josiah W. Smith, B. C. L., of Lincoln's Inn, Barrister at Law. *In 12mo.* (1846.) *Price 5s. boards.*

WATKINS' PRINCIPLES OF CONVEYANCING.
Principles of Conveyancing, designed for the Use of Students, with an Introduction on the Study of that Branch of Law. By Charles Watkins, Esq., Barrister at Law. Revised and considerably enlarged, by Henry Hopley White, Esq., Barrister at Law. *Ninth Edition.*
In 8vo. (1845.) *Price 18s. boards.*

LEWIS ON PERPETUITY.

A PRACTICAL TREATISE on the LAW of PERPETUITY; or Remoteness in Limitations of Estates, as applicable to the various modes of Settlement of Property, Real and Personal, and in its bearing on the different modifications of Ownership in such Property. By William David Lewis, of Lincoln's Inn, Esq., Barrister at Law. *In 8vo.* (1843.) *Price 1l. 6s. boards.*

A SUPPLEMENT to the above, comprising all the Authorities bearing upon the subject of the original Work since its publication.

In 8vo. (1849.) *Price 5s. boards.*

FEARNE'S CONTINGENT REMAINDERS.

An ESSAY on the LEARNING of CONTINGENT REMAINDERS and EXECU-TORY DEVISES. By Charles Fearne, Esq., Barrister at Law, of the Inner Temple. Tenth Edition, containing the Notes, Cases, and other Matter added to the former Editions. By Charles Butler, Esq., of Lincoln's Inn, Barrister at Law. With an Original View of Executory Interests in Real and Personal Property. By Josiah W. Smith, B. C. L., of Lincoln's Inn, Barrister at Law.

In 2 vols. royal 8vo. (1844.) *Price 2l. 4s. boards.*

THE STANNARIES OF CORNWALL.

The CASE of VICE *v.* THOMAS, determined on Appeal before the Lord Warden of the Stannaries of Cornwall, with an Appendix of Records and Documents, illustrating the early History of the Tin Mines of Cornwall, and explanatory Notes. By E. Smirke, M. A., Barrister at Law.

In 8vo. (1843.) *Price 10s. 6d. boards.*

HINTS FOR STUDENTS.

HINTS for STUDENTS at LAW. By a Barrister. *Price 1s.*

PRIOR ON "ISSUE."

A TREATISE on the LAW of CONSTRUCTION of LIMITATIONS in which the Words "ISSUE" and "CHILD" occur; and on the Statute 1 Victoria, c. 26, s. 29. By J. V. Prior, Esq., of the Middle Temple, Barrister at Law.

In 12mo. (1839.) *Price 7s. boards.*

COPYHOLD PROPERTY.

A TREATISE on the LAW of COPYHOLD PROPERTY, with Reference to the various Alterations effected by the Act for the Amendment of the Laws with respect to Wills, and other recent Statutes applicable thereto; with an Appendix, containing the above Act, and an Analysis thereof; and some Forms of Copyhold Assurances. By Henry Stalman, Esq., Barrister at Law.

In 8vo. (1837.) *Price 8s. boards.*

The COPYHOLD ACT, 4 & 5 Victoria, c. 35, and an Analysis of the Act. Edited by H. Stalman, Esq., and intended as a Supplement to the above.

In 8vo. (1841.) *Price 5s. boards.*

CRUISE'S DIGEST OF THE LAW OF REAL PROPERTY.

CRUISE's DIGEST of the LAWS of ENGLAND respecting REAL PROPERTY. The Fourth Edition, revised and considerably enlarged, comprising References throughout the Work to the principal Decisions and to the various important Acts affecting the Law of Real Property, since the former edition in 1824, up to the time of publication, together with a New Chapter on Merger. By Henry Hopley White, Esq., Barrister at Law.

In 7 vols, royal 8vo. (1835.) *Price 5l. 12s. boards.*

COOTE ON MORTGAGE.

A TREATISE on the LAW of MORTGAGE. By Richard Holmes Coote, Esq., of Lincoln's Inn, Barrister at Law.

Third Edition, in royal 8vo. In the Press.

MERCANTILE LAW, RAILWAYS, ETC.

BURGE ON THE LAW OF SURETYSHIP.
COMMENTARIES on the LAW of SURETYSHIP, and the Rights and Obligations of the Parties thereto; and herein of Obligations in Solido under the Laws of England, Scotland, and other States of Europe, the British Colonies and United States of America, and on the Conflict of those Laws. By W. Burge, Esq., of the Inner Temple, One of Her Majesty's Counsel, M. A., Hon. D. C. L. *In 8vo.* (1849.) *Price 18s. boards.*

CARRIERS OF GOODS AND PASSENGERS.
A TREATISE on the LAW of CARRIERS of GOODS and PASSENGERS, by LAND and by WATER. By Joseph K. Angell, Barrister at Law (Boston.) *In royal 8vo.* (1849.) *Price 1l. 5s. boards.*

STURGEON'S BANKRUPTCY ACT.
BANKRUPTCY CONSOLIDATION ACT of 1849; with Practical Notes. By Charles Sturgeon, of the Inner Temple, Esq., Barrister at Law. *In 12mo.* (1849.) *Price 9s. boards.*

BAYLEY ON BILLS.
SUMMARY of the LAW of BILLS of EXCHANGE, CASH BILLS, and PROMISSORY NOTES. By Sir John Bayley, Knt., late one of the Justices of His Majesty's Court of King's Bench. The Sixth Edition. By George Morley Dowdeswell, of the Inner Temple, Esq., Barrister at Law. *In 8vo.* (1849.) *Price 1l. 2s. boards.*

CONTRACTS.—ENGLAND AND SCOTLAND.
A TREATISE on the DIFFERENCES in the LAW of ENGLAND and SCOTLAND as to CONTRACTS affecting PROPERTY; including, Mercantile Contracts, Bailments, Marriage, and Marriage Settlements. By William James Tayler, Esq., of the Inner Temple, Barrister at Law. *In 8vo.* (1849.) *Price 18s. boards.*

ADDISON ON CONTRACTS.
A TREATISE on the LAW of CONTRACTS and RIGHTS and LIABILITIES, ex contractu. By C. G. Addison, Esq., of the Inner Temple, Barrister at Law. *Second Edition, in 2 vols, royal 8vo.* (1849.) *Price 1l. 16s. boards.*

RUSSELL ON AWARDS.
A TREATISE on the POWER and DUTY of an ARBITRATOR, and the LAW of SUBMISSIONS and AWARDS, with an Appendix of Forms, and of the Statutes relating to Arbitration. By Francis Russell, Esq., M. A., Barrister at Law. *In royal 8vo.* (1849.) *Price 1l. 6s. boards.*

SMITH'S MERCANTILE LAW.
A COMPENDIUM of MERCANTILE LAW. By John William Smith, of the Inner Temple, Esq., Barrister at Law. Fourth Edition. By G. M. Dowdeswell, Esq., of the Inner Temple, Barrister at Law. *In royal 8vo.* (1848.) *Price 1l. 12s. boards.*

ARNOULD ON MARINE INSURANCE AND AVERAGE.
A TREATISE on the LAW of MARINE INSURANCE and AVERAGE, with References to the American Cases, and the later Continental Authorities. By Joseph Arnould, Esq., of the Middle Temple, Barrister at Law, and late Fellow of Wadham College, Oxford. *In 2 vols, royal 8vo.* (1848.) *Price 2l. 10s. boards.*

BROOKE'S OFFICE OF A NOTARY.

A TREATISE on the OFFICE and PRACTICE of a NOTARY of ENGLAND, as connected with Mercantile Instruments, and on the Law Merchant, and Statutes relative to the Presentment, Acceptance, and Dishonour of Bills of Exchange, &c., and to various Documents relating to Shipping, with a full Collection of Precedents. Second Edition, with Alterations and Additions. By Richard Brooke, Esq., F. S. A. *In 8vo.* (1848.) *Price 1l. 1s. boards.*

CHAMBERS AND PETERSON ON RAILWAYS.

A TREATISE on the LAW of RAILWAY COMPANIES, in their Formation, Incorporation, and Government, with an Abstract of the Statutes, and a Table of Forms. By Thomas Chambers and A. T. T. Peterson, Esqs., of the Middle Temple, Barristers at Law. *In 8vo.* (1848.) *Price 1l. 4s. boards.*

ABBOTT ON SHIPPING.

A TREATISE of the LAW relative to MERCHANT SHIPS and SEAMEN. In Five Parts. By Charles Lord Tenterden, late Chief Justice of England. The Eighth Edition. By William Shee, Serjeant at Law.
In royal 8vo. (1847.)   *Price 1l. 12s. boards.*

COLLIER'S RAILWAY ACTS.

The RAILWAY CLAUSES, COMPANIES' CLAUSES, and LANDS' CLAUSES CONSOLIDATION ACTS; with Notes, together with an Appendix, treating of the Formation of a Railway Company, the Mode of passing a Bill through Parliament, &c., and an Addenda of Statutes and Forms. By R. P. Collier, of the Inner Temple, Esq., Barrister at Law. The Second Edition, containing the most recent Decisions and the Statutes passed in the Session 9 & 10 Victoria. By H. T. J. Macnamara, of Lincoln's Inn, Esq., Special Pleader.
In 12mo. (1847.)   *Price 14s. boards.*

TAYLOR ON JOINT STOCK COMPANIES.

A PRACTICAL TREATISE on the ACT for the REGISTRATION, REGULATION, and INCORPORATION of JOINT STOCK COMPANIES, 7 & 8 Vict. c. 110 (as amended by 10 & 11 Vict. c. 78), with Directions for the provisional and complete Registration of Companies; intended as a Guide to Persons concerned in the Formation and Management of Companies towards compliance with the Provisions of the Registration Act. To which is added a PRECEDENT of a DEED of SETTLEMENT, prepared and settled in conformity with the provisions of the Act. By George Taylor, Writer to the Signet, Assistant Registrar of Joint Stock Companies. *In 8vo.* (1847.) *Price 14s. boards.*

BISSETT ON PARTNERSHIP.

A PRACTICAL TREATISE on the LAW of PARTNERSHIP; including the Law relating to Railway and other Joint Stock Companies, with an Appendix of Precedents, Forms and Statutes. By Andrew Bisset, of Lincoln's Inn, Esq., Barrister at Law. *In 8vo.* (1847.) *Price 18s. boards.*

SMITH ON CONTRACTS.

The LAW of CONTRACTS, in a COURSE of LECTURES delivered at the LAW INSTITUTION. By John William Smith, Esq., late of the Inner Temple, Barrister at Law, Author of "A Treatise on Mercantile Law," &c. With Notes and Appendix. By Jelinger C. Symons, Esq., of the Middle Temple, Barrister at Law. *In 8vo.* (1847.) *Price 13s. boards.*

RIDDELL'S RAILWAY PRACTICE.

RAILWAY PARLIAMENTARY PRACTICE, with an APPENDIX, containing the Standing Orders of both Houses of Parliament relating to Railways, &c.; to which is added, a Treatise on the Rights of Parties to oppose the Preamble and Clauses of a Railway Bill, and to the Insertion therein of Protective and Compensatory Clauses. By Henry Riddell, Esq., of the Middle Temple, Barrister at Law. *In 12mo.* (1846.) *Price 10s. boards.*

ELLIS ON INSURANCE.

The LAW of FIRE and LIFE INSURANCE and ANNUITIES, with PRACTICAL OBSERVATIONS. Part I. The Law of Fire Insurance   Part II. The Law of Life Insurance.   Part III. The Law of Annuities.   By Charles Ellis, Esq., of Lincoln's Inn, Barrister at Law.   The Second Edition, revised and enlarged. *In 8vo.* (1846.) *Price 10s. boards.*

DOWDESWELL ON INSURANCE.

The LAW of LIFE and FIRE INSURANCE, with an Appendix of Comparative Tables of Life Insurance. By George Morley Dowdeswell, Esq., of the Inner Temple, Barrister at Law. *In 12mo.* (1846.) *Price 6s. boards.*

HINDMARCH ON PATENTS.

A TREATISE on the LAW relating to PATENT PRIVILEGES for the sole use of Inventions, and the Practice of obtaining Letters Patent for Inventions, with an Appendix of Statutes, Rules, Forms, &c. &c. By W. M. Hindmarch, Esq., Barrister at Law. *In 8vo.* (1846.) *Price 1l. 1s. boards.*

RAILWAY LIABILITIES.

As they affect Subscribers, Committees, Allottees, and Scripholders *inter se,* and Third Parties. By J. C. Symons, Esq., Barrister at Law. *Price 2s. 6d.*

KENNEDY ON ANNUITIES.

A TREATISE on ANNUITIES, with an Appendix, containing the Statutes on the Subject. By C. R. Kennedy, Esq., Barrister at Law. *Price 2s. 6d.* (1846.)

GREENWOOD ON LOAN SOCIETIES.

The LAW of LOAN SOCIETIES, established under the Statute 3 & 4 Victoria, c. 110. By John Greenwood, M. A., Barrister at Law. *Price 2s. 12mo.* (1846.)

WORDSWORTH'S JOINT STOCK COMPANIES.

The LAW of RAILWAY, BANKING, MINING, CANAL, and other JOINT STOCK COMPANIES; including the Law relating to the Transfer of Shares, Actions for Calls, Compensations, Bankruptcy of Companies, Remedies in Equity, by Injunction and otherwise; with an Appendix, containing all the Statutes, including those of the last Session, for England, Scotland and Ireland; Forms of Parliamentary and Subscription Contracts, general Forms in Use by Railway Companies, Deeds of Settlement, and other Forms for Banking, Mining, and other Companies; Forms of Pleadings, &c. &c. By Charles Wordsworth, Esq., of the Inner Temple, Barrister at Law.
Fifth Edition, in 8vo. (1845.) *Price 1l. 6s. boards.*

BLACKBURN ON CONTRACTS.

A TREATISE on the EFFECT of the CONTRACT of SALE on the Legal Rights of Property and Possession in Goods, Wares, and Merchandise. By Colin Blackburn, of the Inner Temple, Esq., Barrister at Law.
In 8vo. (1845.) *Price 12s. boards.*

HILDYARD ON MARINE INSURANCE.

A TREATISE on the PRINCIPLES of the LAW of MARINE INSURANCES. By Francis Hildyard, M. A., of the Inner Temple, Esq., Barrister at Law. *In royal 8vo.* (1845.) *Price 1l. 10s. boards.*

BILLING ON AWARDS AND ARBITRATIONS.

A PRACTICAL TREATISE on the LAW of AWARDS and ARBITRATIONS, with Forms of Pleadings, Submissions, and Awards. By Sidney Billing, Esq., Barrister at Law. *In 8vo.* (1845.) *Price 14s. boards.*

BILLING AND PRINCE ON PATENTS.

The LAW and PRACTICE of PATENTS and REGISTRATIONS of DESIGNS, with the Pleadings and all the necessary Forms. By Sidney Billing, of the Middle Temple, Esq., Barrister at Law, and Alexander Prince, of the Office for Patents of Inventions, &c. *In 8vo.* (1845.) *Price 12s. boards.*

COMPOSITION WITH CREDITORS.

A TREATISE on the LAW relating to COMPOSITION with CREDITORS, with an Appendix, containing Precedents of Pleadings and Deeds. By William Forsyth, Esq., M. A., Barrister at Law.
Second Edition, 8vo. (1844.) *Price 9s. boards.*

GODSON ON PATENTS AND COPYRIGHTS.

A PRACTICAL TREATISE on the LAW of PATENTS for INVENTIONS and of COPYRIGHT, illustrated with Notes of the Principal Cases; with an Abstract of the Laws in Force in Foreign Countries. Second Edition. To which is added a Supplement containing the Law to the Present Time. By Richard Godson, M. A., M. P., Barrister at Law. *In 8vo.* (1844.) *Price 1l. 1s. boards.*
The Supplement may be had separately, *price 6s. boards.*

PARK ON MARINE INSURANCE.

A SYSTEM of the LAW of MARINE INSURANCES, with Three Chapters on Bottomry, on Insurances on Lives, and on Insurances against Fire. By Sir James Allan Park, Knight, late one of the Judges of Her Majesty's Court of Common Pleas. By Francis Hildyard, Esq., M. A., of the Inner Temple, Barrister at Law. *Eighth Edition,* 2 vols, *royal 8vo.* (1842). *Price 2l. boards.*

CHITTY'S STAMP LAWS.

A PRACTICAL TREATISE on the STAMP LAWS, with an Appendix of the Statutes, and Notes thereon. By J. Chitty, Esq. Second Edition. By John Walter Hulme, Esq., Barrister at Law. 12mo. (1841.) *Price 12s. boards.*

PRINCIPAL AND AGENT.

A TREATISE on the LAW of PRINCIPAL and AGENT, chiefly with Reference to Mercantile Transactions. By W. Paley, of Lincoln's Inn, Esq., Barrister at Law. With considerable Additions, by J. H. Lloyd, Esq., Barrister at Law. *Third Edition, 8vo.* (1840.) *Price 12s. boards.*

LAW RELATING TO THE PUBLIC FUNDS.

LAW relating to the PUBLIC FUNDS and the Equitable and Legal Remedies with respect to Funded Property; including the Practice by Distringas and under the Statute 1 & 2 Vict. c. 110, with References to the Cases on the Foreign Funds and Public Companies, and an Appendix of Forms. By J. J. Wilkinson, Esq., of Gray's Inn, Special Pleader.
In 12mo. (1839.) *Price 12s. boards.*

HUGHES ON INSURANCE.

A TREATISE on the LAW relating to INSURANCE; *viz.,*—I. Of Marine Insurance. II. Of Insurance of Lives. III. Of Insurance against Fire. By D. Hughes, Esq., Barrister at Law. *In 8vo.* (1828.) *Price 1l. 1s. boards.*

SESSIONS, PARISH LAW, ETC.

PAUPER LUNACY AND ASYLUMS.
The LAW of PAUPER LUNACY, and PAUPER LUNATIC ASYLUMS, as contained in the recent Statutes relating thereto; with an Appendix containing the Criminal Lunatic Acts, Rules for the Selection of Sites of Asylums, and for their Government, and Forms of Treasurers' Accounts. By J. J. Aston, Esq., of the Middle Temple, Barrister at Law. *In* 12mo. (1849.) *Price 5s. boards.*

WOOLRYCH ON SEWERS.
A TREATISE on the LAW of SEWERS, including the Drainage Acts. Second Edition. By H. W. Woolrych, of the Inner Temple, Barrister at Law. *In* 8vo. (1849.) *Price 10s. boards.*

METROPOLITAN SEWERS ACT; with Practical Notes and Comments, with incidental notices of the Nuisance Act, and Metropolitan Buildings Act, for the use of Owners, Occupiers, and Ratepayers. By Charles Tooke, Esq., Barrister at Law. (1849.) *Price 3s. sewed.*

PUBLIC HEALTH, &c.
The PUBLIC HEALTH ACT, 11 & 12 Vict. c. 63, and The NUISANCES REMOVAL ACT, 11 & 12 Vict. c. 123; with Notes and Indexes; being a Companion to the Law of Sewers. By Humphry W. Woolrych, Esq., Barrister at Law. *In* 12mo. (1848.) *Price 5s. boards.*

The PUBLIC HEALTH ACT, and Forms of Petitions, Orders, Informations, Warrants, Notices, Awards, Convictions, and other Proceedings necessary for putting it into Execution; with Explanatory Notes and an Index. By Thomas Howard Fellows, of the Inner Temple, Special Pleader.
In 12mo. (1848.) *Price 5s. boards.*

WOOLRYCH ON WAYS.
A TREATISE of the LAW of WAYS; including Highways, Turnpike Roads and Tolls, Private Right of Way, Bridges and Ferries, with the Law of the Prescription Act, 2 & 3 Wm. 4, c. 71, and of Railways, as far as they relate to Highways and Turnpike Roads. Second Edition. By Humphry W. Woolrych, Esq., of the Inner Temple, Barrister at Law. *In* 8vo. (1847.) *Price 1l. 1s. boards.*

WOOLRYCH ON INCLOSURES.
The NEW INCLOSURE ACT, 8 & 9 Vict. c. 118; with Notes and Indexes. By H. W. Woolrych, Esq., Barrister at Law. *In* 8vo. (1846.) *Price 6s. boards.*

PAUPER LUNATICS.
The PAUPER LUNATIC ASYLUM ACT, (8 & 9 Vict. c. 126), with an Analysis of its Provisions, Explanatory Notes, and a Copious Index. By J. F. Pownall, of Lincoln's Inn, Esq., Barrister at Law. *In* 8vo. (1845). *Price 4s. boards.*

PARTY WALLS AND FENCES.
The LAW of PARTY WALLS and FENCES, including the New Metropolitan Buildings Act, with Notes. By H. W. Woolrych, of the Inner Temple, Esq., Barrister at Law. *In 8vo.* (1844.) *Price 12s. boards.*

STEER'S PARISH LAW.
PARISH LAW; being a Digest of the Law relating to Parishes, Churches and Chapels, Parish Registers, Ministers of Churches and Chapels, Vestries and Parish Meetings, Churchwardens, Parish Clerks, Sextons and Beadles, Dissenters, Highways, Parish and County Rates, Watching and Lighting Parishes, Weights and Measures, Disorderly Houses, Militia and Jury List, Justices of the Peace, Constables, Watchmen, &c., Vagrants, Lunatics, Overseers, Guardians, Settlement, Friendly Societies, &c., and the Relief, Settlement, and removal of the Poor. Second Edition. By G. Clive, Esq., Barrister at Law, late Assistant Poor Law Commissioner.
Second Edition, in 8vo. (1843.) *Price 1l. 4s. boards.*

RIGHTS OF COMMON.
A TREATISE on the LAW of RIGHTS of COMMON, with a Supplement containing the new Cases and Statutes to the present time. By H. W. Woolrych, Esq., Barrister at Law. *In 8vo.* (1835.) *Price 15s. boards.* The Supplement may be had separately, *price 1s.*

WATERS AND SEWERS.
A TREATISE on the LAW of WATERS and SEWERS; including the Law relating to Rights in the Sea, and Rights in Rivers, Canals, Dock Companies, Fisheries, Mills, Watercourses, User of Rights connected with Water, Obstruction and other Injuries, with Remedies in such Cases. Extinguishment, Suspension, Revivor. Incidents to Rights connected with Water. Indictments and Pleadings, Evidence, &c. Of Commission of Sewers, and their Origin. Of the Duties and Powers of Commissioners of Sewers. Of the Proceedings of Commissioners of Sewers in Furtherance of the Powers intrusted to them. Of the various Proceedings which may be had against Commissioners of Sewers, and Forms of Precedents, with a Supplement containing the Cases and Statutes to 1834. By H. W. Woolrych, Esq., Barrister at Law. The Supplement may be had separately, *price 2s. In 8vo.* (1834.) *Price 18s. boards.*

ARCHBOLD'S QUARTER SESSIONS.
The JURISDICTION and PRACTICE of the COURT of QUARTER SESSIONS. With Forms of Indictments, Notices of Appeal, &c. By John Frederick Archbold, Esq., Barrister at Law. *In 12mo.* (1836). *Price 14s. boards.*

COMMITMENTS AND CONVICTIONS.
ARCHBOLD'S (J. F.) LAW relative to COMMITMENTS and CONVICTIONS, by Justices of the Peace, with Forms; to which are added Lord Lansdowne's Acts. *In 12mo.* (1828.) *Price 14s. 6d. boards.*

ECCLESIASTICAL LAW, ETC.

ROGERS'S ECCLESIASTICAL LAW.
A Practical Arrangement of ECCLESIASTICAL LAW. By Francis Newman Rogers, Esq., Barrister at Law, Recorder of Exeter, and Deputy Judge Advocate General. *Second Edition, considerably enlarged.* (1849.) *Price 1l. 16s. boards.*

HAMPDEN CASE.
A Report of the CASE of the Right Rev. R. D. HAMPDEN, D.D., Lord Bishop Elect of Hereford, in Hereford Cathedral, the Ecclesiastical Courts, and the Queen's Bench, with the Judgments and Arguments authenticated; the Records and Documents in full, and a copious Index. By Richard Jebb, Esq., A.M., of Lincoln's Inn, Barrister at Law. *In royal 8vo. Price 12s. boards.*

WADDILOVE'S DIGEST.
A DIGEST of CASES decided in the Court of Arches, the Prerogative Court of Canterbury, and the Consistory Court of London, and on Appeal therefrom to the Judicial Committee of the Privy Council; with References to the leading analagous Decisions in the House of Lords, and the Courts of Law and Equity, and to the several Statutes and Text Books which bear on Questions within the Jurisdiction of the Ecclesiastical Courts. By Alfred Waddilove, D. C. L., Advocate in Doctors' Commons, and Barrister at Law of the Inner Temple. *In royal 8vo.* (1849.) *Price 1l. 5s. boards.*

WILLIAMS ON EXECUTORS.
A TREATISE on the LAW of EXECUTORS and ADMINISTRATORS. By Edward Vaughan Williams, of Lincoln's Inn, Esq., Barrister at Law (now one of the Judges of Her Majesty's Court of Common Pleas.)
Fourth Edition. In 2 vols. royal 8vo. (1849.) *Price 3l. 8s. cloth boards.*

LAWS OF THE CLERGY.
A PRACTICAL TREATISE on the LAWS relating to the CLERGY. By Archibald John Stephens, Esq., Barrister at Law.
In 2 vols. royal 8vo. (1848.) *Price 2l. 18s. boards.*

> This publication is intended to supply the clerical and legal professions with a practical Treatise of Clerical Law. The alphabetical arrangement of the subjects has been adopted with a view to convenience of reference.
> The authenticated judgments of Lord Denman, Mr. Justice Patteson, Mr. Justice Coleridge, and Mr. Justice Erle, in *Regina v. Archbishop of Canterbury*, relating to the confirmation of the elections of Bishops, and the opinions of the Court in *Regina v. Chadwick*, as to the legality of a marriage with the sister of a deceased wife will be found, *inter alia*, in the Addenda.

ROPER ON LEGACIES.
A TREATISE on the LAW of LEGACIES. By R. S. Donnison Roper, Esq., Barrister at Law, and by Henry Hopley White, Esq., Barrister at Law, of the Middle Temple.
Fourth Edition. In 2 vols. royal 8vo. (1847.) *Price 3l. 3s. boards.*

PHILLIMORE ON DOMICIL.
The LAW of DOMICIL. By Robert Phillimore, Esq., Advocate in Doctors' Commons, and Barrister at Law. *In 8vo.* (1847.) *Price 9s. boards.*

LAW'S CHURCH BUILDING ACTS.

The ACTS for BUILDING and PROMOTING of additional CHURCHES in populous Parishes, arranged and harmonized with a Preamble, Appendix, and Index. By James T. Law, A.M., late Special Commissary of the Diocese of Bath and Wells. *In 8vo.* (1847.) *Price 6s. boards.*

EDWARDS'S ABRIDGMENT OF THE WILLS' ACT.

ABRIDGMENT of CASES in the Prerogative Court, under the New Statute of Wills, 1 Vict. c. 26, being a Digest of all the Decisions thereon in that Court, and arranged under the Sections to which they apply respectively; with Notes and Index, intended as a Work of Reference and Practice, with respect to the Execution of Wills. By Edwin Edwards, Esq., of Doctors' Commons. *In 12mo.* (1846.) *Price 5s. boards.*

BILLING ON PEWS.

The LAWS relating to PEWS in Churches, District Churches, Chapels, and Proprietary Chapels, the Rights incidental thereto, and the Remedy for Wrongs. By Sidney Billing, Esq., of the Middle Temple, Barrister at Law. *In 8vo.* (1845.) *Price 8s. boards.*

STONE ALTAR CASE.

The JUDGMENT of the Right Hon. Sir H. J. FUST, in the Case of FAULKNER *v.* LITCHFIELD. Edited from the Judge's Notes by J. E. P. Robertson, D. C. L., Advocate. *In 8vo.* (1845.) *Price 3s. sewed.*

OAKELEY'S CASE.

A Full Report of the Proceedings in the Case of the Office of the Judge Promoted by HODGSON *v.* REV. F. OAKELEY, before the Right Hon. Sir H. J. Fust, Knt., Dean of the Arches, &c. &c. Edited by A. F. Bayford, D. C. L., Advocate. *In 8vo.* (1845.) *Price 6s. boards.*

LAW'S ECCLESIASTICAL FORMS.

FORMS of ECCLESIASTICAL LAW; the Mode of Conducting Suits in the Consistory Courts, being a Translation of the First Part of Oughton's Ordo Judiciorum, with large Additions from Clarke's Praxis, Conset's Praxis, Ayliffe's Parergon, Cockburn's Clerk's Assistant, Gibson's Codex, &c. By James T. Law, A.M. *Second Edition, 8vo.* (1844.) *Price 15s. boards.*

FORSYTH ON SIMONY.

The LAW Relating to SIMONY considered with a View to its Revision. By William Forsyth, Esq., M.A., Barrister at Law. *In 8vo.* (1844.) *Price 2s. 6d.*

EAGLE'S TITHE ACTS.

The Acts for the COMMUTATION of TITHES in England and Wales, 6 & 7 Wm. 4, c. 71; 1 Vict. c. 69; 1 & 2 Vict. c. 74; 2 & 3 Vict. c. 62; 3 Vict. c. 15; and 5 & 6 Vict. c. 54, with Notes, Appendix, and Index. By William Eagle, Esq., Barrister at Law. *Third Edition, 12mo.* (1840.) *Price 8s. boards.*

The CONSTITUTIONS of OTHO and OTHOBON, with Notes. By J. W. White, Esq., of Doctors' Commons, Proctor. *Price 2s. 6d. sewed.*

GWYNNE'S PROBATE DUTIES.

The LAW relating to the DUTIES on PROBATES and LETTERS of ADMINIS-
TRATION in England, and Inventories of Personal or Moveable Estates in
Scotland, and on Legacies and Successions to Personal or Moveable Estates in
Great Britain : also the Rules and Practice of the Legacy Duty Office in London,
and correct Copies of the Forms used in the Department, with Instructions for
filling them up. To which is added a Summary of the adjudicated Cases,
classed under separate heads, and with References to the published Reports
thereof. By Thomas Gwynne, Esq., Comptroller of the said Duties.
Third Edition, 8vo. (1838.) *Price* 10s. *boards.*

TOLLER ON EXECUTORS.

The LAW of EXECUTORS and ADMINISTRATORS By Sir Samuel Toller,
Knight, late Advocate General of Madras. Corrected, with considerable
Additions. By Francis Whitmarsh, Esq., one of Her Majesty's Counsel.
Seventh Edition, 8vo. (1838.) *Price* 16s. *boards.*

ROBERTS ON WILLS.

A TREATISE on the LAW of WILLS and CODICILS, including the Construction of Devises, and the Duties of Executors and Administrators; with
an Appendix of Precedents. Much enlarged and improved. By W. Roberts,
Esq. *Third Edition.* 2 vols. royal 8vo. (1837.) *Price* 2l. 5s. *boards.*

A SUPPLEMENT to the Treatise on Wills and Codicils, exhibiting the
effects of the Decision of the Courts since the Publication of that work,
and especially the Alterations introduced by the Statute, 1 Vict. c. 26. By
William Roberts, of Lincoln's Inn, Esq., Barrister at Law.
In royal 8vo. (1837.) *Price* 6s. *boards.*

LANDLORD AND TENANT, ETC.

LAW OF FIXTURES.

A TREATISE on the LAW of FIXTURES, and other PROPERTY partaking both
of a REAL and PERSONAL NATURE ; comprising the Law relating to Annex-
ations to the Freehold in general; as also Emblements, Charters, Heirlooms,
&c., with an Appendix, containing Practical Rules and Directions respecting
the Removal, Purchase, Valuation, &c. of Fixtures between Landlord and
Tenant, and between outgoing and incoming Tenants. By A. Amos, Esq., and
J. Ferard, Esq., Barristers at Law. The Second Edition. By Joseph Ferard,
Esq., Barrister at Law. *In royal* 8vo. (1847.) *Price* 16s. *boards.*

ADAMS (MR. SERJT.) ON EJECTMENT.

A TREATISE on the Principles and Practice of the ACTION of EJECTMENT,
and the Resulting ACTION for MESNE PROFITS. The Fourth Edition, with
considerable Additions, by John Adams, Serjeant at Law.
In royal 8vo. (1846.) *Price* 18s. *boards.*

COOTE'S LANDLORD AND TENANT LAW.

A TREATISE on the LAW of LANDLORD and TENANT; grounded on the
Text of COMYN, and embracing the important parts of WOODFALL and
CHAMBERS. By Richard Holmes Coote, Esq., Barrister at Law.
In royal 8vo. (1840.) *Price* 1l. 1s. *boards.*

ADMIRALTY.

PRITCHARD'S ADMIRALTY DIGEST.

An Analytical DIGEST of all the REPORTED CASES determined by the High Court of Admiralty of England, the Lords Commissioners of Appeal in Prize Causes, and (on Questions of Maritime and International Law) by the Judicial Committee of the Privy Council; also of the analogous Cases in the Common Law, Equity, and Ecclesiastical Courts, and of the Statutes applicable to the Cases reported. With Notes from the Text Writers and other authorities on Maritime Law, and the Scotch, Irish, and American Reports; and an Appendix containing the principal Statutes, &c. &c. By William Tarn Pritchard, one of the Proctors of the Ecclesiastical and Admiralty Courts in Doctors' Commons. *In royal 8vo.* (1847.) *Price 1l. 10s. boards.*

EDWARDS'S ADMIRALTY JURISDICTION.

A TREATISE on the Jurisdiction of the High Court of Admiralty of England. By Edwin Edwards, Esq., of Doctors' Commons. *In 8vo.* (1847.) *Price 10s. boards.*

PIRACY.

The Case of The QUEEN *v.* SERVA and Others, inclusive of the Trial and the Argument before the Judges. By W. B. Hewson, Esq., Barrister at Law. *In 8vo.* (1846.) *Price 3s. 6d.*

CRIMINAL LAW.

ROSCOE'S CRIMINAL EVIDENCE.

A DIGEST of the LAW of EVIDENCE in Criminal Cases. By Henry Roscoe, Esq., of the Inner Temple, Barrister at Law. Third Edition, with considerable Additions. By T. C. Granger, Esq., Barrister at Law.
In royal 12mo. (1846.) *Price 1l. 5s. boards.*

RUSSELL ON CRIMES AND MISDEMEANORS.

A TREATISE on CRIMES and MISDEMEANORS. By Sir William Oldnall Russell, Knight, late Chief Justice of Bengal. By Charles Sprengel Greaves, Esq., of Lincoln's Inn and the Inner Temple, Barrister at Law, and a Magistrate for the County of Stafford. Third Edition.
In 2 vols. royal 8vo. (1843.) *Price 4l. boards.*

PEEL'S ACTS.

PEEL'S ACTS, and all the other Criminal Statutes passed from the First year of the Reign of Geo. IV. to the present time; including the Criminal Clauses of the Reform Act, with the Forms of Indictments, &c., and the Evidence necessary to support them. Third Edition, with considerable Additions and Alterations. By John Frederick Archbold, Esq., Barrister at Law. *In 2 vols, 12mo.* (1835.) *Price 1l. 8s. boards.*

PARLIAMENT, ELECTIONS, STATUTES, ETC.

RIDDELL AND ROGERS' INDEX.

An INDEX to the PUBLIC STATUTES, from 9 Hen. 3 to 10 & 11 Vict. inclusive (excepting those relating exclusively to Scotland, Ireland, the Colonies and Dependencies), analytically arranged, and affording a synoptical View of the Statute Book. By Henry Riddell and John Warrington Rogers, Esqrs., of the Middle Temple, Barristers at Law. Part the First.
In royal 8vo. (1848.) *Price 1l. 1s. boards.* (Part II. will be published shortly.)

DWARRIS (SIR F.) ON THE STATUTES.

A General TREATISE on STATUTES; their rules of Construction and the proper Boundaries of Legislation and of judicial Interpretation, including a Summary of the Practice of Parliament, and the ancient and modern Method of Proceeding in passing Bills of every Kind. Part the First: Constitutional and Parliamentary. Part the Second: Legal. Second Edition. By Sir Fortunatus Dwarris, Knt., B.A., Oxford, F.R.S., F.S.A., assisted by W. H. Amyot, Esq., Barrister at Law. *In 8vo.* (1848.) *Price 1l. 10s. boards.*

WORDSWORTH'S REGISTRATION ACTS.

The LAW relating to the REGISTRATION of VOTERS, including the Practice and Decisions of the Court of Common Pleas on Appeals, with the Statute 6 Vict. c. 18, and various Forms. By Charles Wordsworth, Esq. of the Inner Temple, Barrister at Law. *Third Edition, in 8vo.* (1845.) *Price 6s. boards.*

LUTWYCHE'S REGISTRATION CASES.

REPORTS of CASES argued and determined in the Court of Common Pleas on Appeals from the Decisions of the Revising Barristers, from Michaelmas Term, 1843, to Hilary Term, 1847. By A. J. P. Lutwyche, of the Middle Temple, Esq., Barrister at Law. Vol. 1. *In royal 8vo. Price 1l. 11s. 6d. sewed.*

Vol. 2, Parts 1 and 2, Michaelmas Term, 1847, Michaelmas Term, 1848. *Price 8s. sewed.*

CHAMBERS' DICTIONARY OF ELECTIONS.

A COMPLETE DICTIONARY of the LAW and PRACTICE of Elections of Members of Parliament, and of Election Petitions and Committees for England, Scotland, and Ireland, compiled from the Journals, Reports, Treatises, Minutes, and Statutes, from the earliest period. By John David Chambers, M.A., Barrister at Law. *In 8vo.* (1837.) *Price 1l. 5s. boards.*

WORDSWORTH ON ELECTIONS.

The LAW and PRACTICE of ELECTIONS and Election Petitions, with all the Statutes and Forms. Third Edition. By Charles Wordsworth, Esq., of the Inner Temple, Barrister at Law. *In 8vo.* (1847.) *Price 1l. 4s. boards.*

JURISPRUDENCE, TRIALS, ETC.

INTERNATIONAL LAW.
INSTITUTES of INTERNATIONAL LAW. By Richard Wildman, Esq., of the Inner Temple, Barrister at Law; Recorder of Nottingham, &c. Vol. I. International Rights in Time of Peace. *In 8vo.* (1849.) *Price 7s. 6d. boards.*

ROMAN CIVIL LAW.
A SUMMARY of the ROMAN CIVIL LAW, illustrated by Commentaries on and Parallels from the Mosaic, Canon, Mohammedan, English and Foreign Law. By Patrick Colquhoun, Esq. *In 8vo.* Part I. *Price 10s. 6d.*
Part II., preparing for the Press.

ROMAN LAW.
INTRODUCTION to the STUDY and HISTORY of the ROMAN LAW. By John George Phillimore. *In 8vo.* (1848.) *Price 15s. boards.*

CELEBRATED TRIALS.
CELEBRATED TRIALS, connected with the Aristocracy in the Relations of Private Life. By Peter Burke, Esq., of the Inner Temple, Barrister at Law. *In 8vo.* (1848.) *Price 16s. cloth boards.*

"Mr. Burke has collected these trials in one volume, which may safely be pronounced one of the most curious and interesting ever published."—*Morning Post.* "This is a very interesting book. There are few, very few, cases in it that will not be read with great interest, or that will not be found filled with details more strange than novelist or romance writer has ever ventured to combine together in a pure and professed work of fiction."—*Morning Herald.* "The volume altogether is just one of those which Mr. Warren, we fancy, would commend to the particular attention of legal students, from its combination of strange facts and legal subtlety." —*Britannia.* "It is impossible to overrate the importance of these trials as illustrations of the history of our country."—*Liverpool Chronicle.*

DUTIES OF ATTORNIES AND SOLICITORS.
The MORAL, SOCIAL, and PROFESSIONAL DUTIES of ATTORNIES and SOLICITORS. By Samuel Warren, Esq., F.R.S., of the Inner Temple, Barrister at Law. (1848.) *Price 9s. cloth boards.*

CODE NAPOLEON,
Or, the FRENCH CIVIL CODE, literally Translated by a Barrister of the Inner Temple. *In royal 8vo.* (1827.) *Price 1l. 1s. boards.*

JURISPRUDENCE.
On JURISPRUDENCE, with an Historical Essay on the Law of Evidence. By J. G. Phillimore, Esq. Preparing for the Press.

Law Reports.

———◆———

	£	s.	d.
QUEEN'S BENCH REPORTS.			
ADOLPHUS & ELLIS, 12 vols, from 1834 to 1840 -	19	9	0
——————— (new series), 8 vols, from 1840 to 1845 -	16	17	0
——————— vol 9, parts 1 to 4, Trinity Term and Vacation, 1846, and Hilary, 1847 - - - -	2	1	0
——————— vol 10, parts 1, 2, and 3, Trinity and Hilary Vacation, 1847 - - - - -	1	17	6
These Reports will be regularly continued.			
COMMON BENCH REPORTS.			
MANNING & GRANGER, 7 vols, East. 1840 to Mich. 1844 -	15	18	6
MANNING, GRANGER, & SCOTT, vols 1 to 5, Hil. 1845 to East. 1848	10	19	6
——————— vol 6, part 1, East. & Mich. 1848	0	7	0
These Reports will be regularly continued.			
CROWN CASES RESERVED.			
DENISON, part 1 to 4, Mich. 1844 to Trin. 1849 -	0	13	6
These Reports will be continued.			
HIGH COURT OF CHANCERY.			
PHILLIPS, 2 vols, from 1842 to 1848 - - -	4	7	6
MACNAGHTEN & GORDON, parts 1 and 2, 1849 -	0	12	6
These Reports will be regularly continued.			
ROLLS' COURT.			
BEAVAN, 10 vols, from 1838 to 1847 - - -	16	0	0
These Reports will be regularly continued.			
ECCLESIASTICAL COURT.			
ROBERTSON (J. E. P.), D.C.L., parts 1, 2, and 3, 1844 to 1847	1	11	6
SESSIONS CASES.			
CARROW, HAMILTON, & ALLEN, 2 vols, Hil. 1844 to Trin. 1847 -	3	16	0
HAMERTON, ALLEN, & OTTER, vol 3, parts 1 to 6, Mich. 1847 to Trinity, 1849 - - - - -	1	11	0
These Reports will be regularly continued.			
BAIL COURT REPORTS.			
SAUNDERS & COLE, 2 vols, Hil. 1846 to Mich. 1848 -	2	0	0

=========

A Large Collection of Private and Local Acts.

The Reports, Statutes, and Periodicals supplied on the Day of Publication.

Law Libraries bought or valued.

[PRINTED BY RAYNER AND HODGES, 109, Fetter Lane, Fleet Street.

www.ingramcontent.com/pod-product-compliance
Lightning Source LLC
Chambersburg PA
CBHW071152050326
40689CB00011B/2086